SHE RODE A HARLEY

A MEMOIR OF LOVE AND MOTORCYCLES

MARY JANE BLACK

She Writes Press, a BookSparks imprint
A Division of SparkPointStudio, LLC.

Published 2019
Printed in the United States of America

ISBN: 978-1-63152-620-6 pbk
ISBN: 978-1-63152-621-3 ebk
Library of Congress Control Number: 2019940987

For information, address:
She Writes Press
1569 Solano Ave #546
Berkeley, CA 94707

She Writes Press is a division of SparkPoint Studio, LLC.

THE BEGINNING

1995-1999

❧

I'm a believer.

THE MONKEES

HE THINKS
HE'LL KEEP HER

My escape can't happen until Tom finishes his breakfast. While I wait, I pack his lunch the way I have for twenty-three years. I carefully arrange the ham-and-cheese sandwich on the left and exactly twenty-five chips in a bag next to it with a two-inch square of cake in the bottom of the black plastic lunch box. Suddenly the phone rings. It breaks the silence like a shot.

I grab it and say "hello" in the most normal voice I can find. It's the manager of the apartment complex where I have just rented an apartment—the security deposit paid with a secret bank account where, for five years, I hoarded twenties, tens, and fives.

A voice chirps in my year, "Good morning, Mrs. Richards, I just wanted to confirm that you and your daughter are moving in this afternoon." The woman asks if I want to move into a ground-floor apartment or the third-floor one I looked at earlier.

I consider how I can answer this question without raising Tom's suspicions. I shift my body slightly so I can see his face more clearly. He's stopped shoveling eggs into his mouth. The yolks drip from his raised fork onto his plate.

"No, third floor is fine." I finish the sentence in my head. *It's much harder for someone to get through the security door and up three flights of stairs without warning.* She assures me she will be glad to have me join their little community of residents, then tells me how much I'll enjoy Springfield, Missouri. I can't tell her that I already live in a small town near the city, since I want her to see me as a stranger who doesn't know anyone.

I lay the phone gently back on the hook. I return to the sink and start washing a cup, taking a long time.

"Who the hell was that?" He lays down his fork and brings his plate to the sink, standing inches from me. His dark eyes glare into mine. I stare at the patch of pink scalp beneath his thin brown hair.

"It was my principal. He wanted to make sure I was okay with his moving me to a classroom on the third floor next year." For a moment, I feel triumphant in my ability to create a lie so quickly. Then I remember that any slip can be dangerous. I'm an acrobat on the high wire waiting to fall.

Tom studies me. I absorb myself in removing every speck of food on the plates.

He reaches out and jerks my right arm out of the soapy water. His fingers dig into my wrist. He stares at me and clears his throat with a loud rapid hacking. I wonder if he's always done this, or if after the recent tense years, I've noticed it more. Now I flinch at the sound.

I blank out any emotion on my face. Water drips slowly onto the floor. We stand in silence, and the clock behind us ticks away the seconds. Finally, he drops my arm with a flourish. It bangs painfully against the edge of the counter. He steps away from me to avoid getting water on his starched blue shirt.

"Wipe the water off the floor." He walks away.

I stand frozen as I listen to the garage door roll up with a groan. Then I hear his car start and the sound of the motor growing fainter as he pulls out of the driveway. I look out the window over the sink and watch the birds fly and dip over the newly green grass in our back yard. In my head I count off the minutes until it's safe to move.

When enough time has passed, I yell down the stairs to Stephanie to start bringing her stuff up to her car. I help her load her car, shoving boxes and clothes on hangers in every inch of space in the small car. I marvel at how many clothes and shoes a sixteen-year-old girl owns.

I open the driver's door. She hugs me. Her eyes are big with fear but also a little excitement at the idea of joining me in running away. I know it has been hard for her keeping this secret from her father and even her brother. He has never shown any anger toward them. His rage and jealousy are saved for me.

I'll call Steven as soon as I stand safely in our new home. I know how angry my son will be that I have left his father. The last time I tried to leave, I told him in advance. It cost me bruised ribs and a twisted arm.

Now Stephanie climbs into the car and screeches out of the driveway, clothes fluttering in the wind. Thumping music trails behind her as she pulls onto the road and heads to her high school. After we unload the truck, she'll come to our new apartment this afternoon.

Soon my mom and my cousin Bryce swing the top-heavy U-Haul I've secretly rented into the driveway and back it up to the front door. I've stacked the dishes and other things I'll need from the kitchen on the counter.

We develop a rhythm of packing. Wrap in newspaper, place in box. Wrap and place. Wrap and place. Go outside and stack the boxes in the truck. Moving quickly, we soon have everything packed. I'm careful not to take too much. I agonized over whether to take the coffee pot. I do.

I check the clock each time I go in the house to watch the time. Every minute that passes increases the chances of Tom's return home.

"What furniture's going?" Bryce asks.

I list off the furniture we're loading—exactly half of the furniture in the house, but not the bed we shared.

With strength we didn't know we possessed, we load the truck with furniture and boxes in two hours. An added incentive for our speed was finding his packed lunch box in the garage, signaling he is planning on coming home for lunch. He wants to surprise me.

The phone call this morning had not been forgotten. Since my ultimate betrayal of going to college and getting a teaching job six years ago, he's been on watch for other abnormal behavior. I can't think about this now. Time marches forward. My heart beats furiously against my ribs, and I steady myself, placing a hand against the wall until the dizziness passes.

As I finally stand by the loaded truck, Mom hesitates at the truck door as she starts to climb up into the passenger seat.

For fifteen years after my father's suicide, we barely spoke and have only recently begun to feel like mother and child again. I realize in this moment of escape that she was forty-one like me when she left me and her life in our hometown.

Now she reaches out to hold me. I'm folded into the softness of her large, warm body. "Mary, you're going to be behind us, right?" she asks, releasing me.

I nod, since I only have one more job to do. I walk back into the partially empty house and look around me at the rooms where I first came as an eighteen-year-old bride. I knew on that day that I didn't feel the passionate love other brides felt, feeling I had traded that for safety from the battlefield of my parents' marriage. Everything that reflected me has been stripped from the house.

I take a deep breath and remove a letter from its hiding place in the lining of my purse and put it in an envelope. "Tom," I write on the front. Inside the letter in a few sentences I tell him that when he reads this I will be gone. That this is not my home now. I don't ask for his forgiveness. None will be given.

I close and lock the front door for the last time, slipping my key under the doormat. I get in my car and sail out of the driveway. I push in the cassette tape, and Mary Chapin Carpenter sings: "He thinks he'll keep her." I fly out of the driveway into the unknown future.

I'M A BELIEVER

I return home from a long day of teaching to find my daughter gone. I push open the front door and yell for her to help me. Balancing a sack of groceries and a tote bag of student essays to grade, I yell, "Stephanie!"

First once. Silence. Then over and over. No response.

I lay the sack onto the kitchen table by the door and drop the essay bag on the floor. I look down the short hallway into my daughter's room. Her unmade bed is a tangle of sheets and blankets. Piles of discarded clothes on the floor. But she's not there.

Without moving, I can see she's not anywhere in our tiny four-room apartment. I only hope my daughter's absence is due to homework or softball practice. Last week I found her bed vacant in the morning and searched for her for two hours. She had sneaked out to a party while I was sleeping.

As I put up the groceries, I notice the blinking light on the answering machine and push it reluctantly. Tom's voice fills the air. "I hope you haven't forgotten we're supposed to go to marriage counseling tonight. You missed the last one. You need to show up. If you don't follow the court orders, the judge will hear about it." *Beep.*

I hit the delete button. Then I press it four times, pushing harder each time. The mechanized voice tells me the message has been deleted.

Next message. "Hey, Mary. This is Vicky. Tod has a friend from his work in Texas in town for a quick business dinner. How about joining us? He's single." My finger lingers over the delete button this time. Then I push it.

I take a deep breath and tap in Tom's number. He answers the phone after the first ring. "I'm surprised you took the time to call."

I tell him I'm only calling to say I won't be there tonight. He instantly responds, "You don't seem to care about your son and God knows dragging Stephanie off to live in a small apartment shows you don't give a crap about her either."

I swallow my response. I merely repeat I won't be at the counselor's, but I will see him at our court-ordered mediation next week.

He clears his throat into the phone and whispers, "I'll make you pay for this."

I close my eyes and wait for the threat.

On the other end of the line, I hear his labored breathing. "You are dead to me. If I have my way, you'll never see either one of our children again."

I hang up the phone without a sound. Then picking it up again, I bang it down. I didn't want him to know he's gotten to me again.

I dial Vicky's number and start to say I won't be at Chili's at seven to meet some strange Texan. A desperate need to do something reckless for the first time in my life rises in me. A need to do something to prove I'm moving on with my life. I hear my voice say, "I'll see you at seven." I instantly regret my decision.

I track down Stephanie at a friend's house and tell her I won't be home for a couple hours, not telling her I'm meeting a man for dinner.

Briefly contemplating changing my clothes from the sensible pants and shirt I wore to school, I look down at my comfortable loafers. I consider a dress and heels. Maybe even makeup. Teaching high school students grammar and literature all day requires stamina, not a sense of style and fashion. I stare at the clothes in my closet but soon slam the door shut. I used up my energy saying yes to a blind date. I decide Mr. Texas will just have to take me as I am.

I pull into the restaurant parking lot fifteen minutes late to find Vicky standing outside waiting. She sways a little on her stiletto heels as she walks toward me. Her long blond hair hangs perfectly curled across the shoulder of her pale pink designer suit. Unlike me, she is dressed for dinner with a man. She looks at me and frowns. "I thought you weren't going to show up!"

"Hey, it's a free meal. I don't get many of those."

I follow her to the back of the restaurant, and we stop at a booth. A tall man in starched jeans and a turquoise striped shirt stands. He looks at me with dark chocolate eyes. His chestnut hair dips perfectly across his forehead. An ample mustache covers his top lip under a battered nose.

He speaks in a slow drawl. "What took you so long?"

I step closer to him, taking a deep fluttering breath.

In the middle of the crowded restaurant, we stare at each other without speaking. He breaks the silence. "You must be Mary. I'm Dwayne."

He takes my hand, and his broad rough fingers wrap around my hand. Looking into his craggy face, I smile. He grins back and winks. We stand holding hands for a long moment while diners talking and dishes clinking fade into the background. The smell of burgers frying fills the air. The ordinary sounds and smells of a Friday night restaurant fade in the astonishing moment of finding a stranger who's so familiar.

The waitress breaks the connection. My shaking hand on the table pushes me across the hard, smooth seat of the booth. Avoiding Vicky's questioning look across the table, I focus on slowing my breath.

Dwayne slides in by me. Without speaking, we lean into each other. Something I couldn't have imagined doing a few hours ago.

Over dinner Dwayne and Tod talk about their project where Dwayne will be installing elephant crushes at the Cleveland Zoo. Tod laughs and announces that he can design a system for moving elephants, but only Dwayne can build the hydraulics to make it work.

I turn and face Dwayne. "What are elephant crushes?"

He tells me he'll show me how they work, and he arranges salt and pepper shakers and silverware in the middle of the table. Showing how the elephant enters the cage with a push of a spoon between the shakers, he swirls the spoon, so I can see how the hydraulic lift raises the elephant for the vets. As he demonstrates the machine, a carved silver ring on his right hand shines. Without thinking, I rub it with my index finger and ask him about it.

"It's my Harley ring. I've worn it since I was sixteen. That's when I was working at my first Harley shop."

I ask him why he's wearing it upside down. He holds up his hand with his fingers pointing down. "You have to wear a Harley ring with the bar and shield upside down on your finger, so someone can see it the right way when you shake their hand or make a fist."

"Do you own a Harley now?"

"No, my wife made me sell my scooter when my daughter, Jessica, was born."

"Wife?"

"Wife and divorce number two. I like living alone now."

He sips his drink of amber Scotch, no ice. "If I ever get the chance to get another Harley, I'll take you for a ride. You'll be hooked for life." We smile at the promise.

I suddenly remember Vicky and Tod are at the table with us. When I turn away from Dwayne to talk to them, I notice they aren't eating, watching the two of us. Breaking the silence, I ask Vicky about preparation for summer school, starting in a few weeks for us. As we chat about school and students, I am aware of Dwayne's arm lying on the back of the seat, warm against my neck.

Midway through dinner Vicky and I excuse ourselves to go to the bathroom. As soon as we walk in the door, she grabs my elbow. "I've never seen you like this."

I tell her I've never felt like this. "I can't even explain it. I feel protected for the first time ever. Does that even make sense?" I stare at myself in the mirror and see a wide-eyed happy stranger staring back. "Home. I feel like I came home at last."

As we walk back to our table, Vicky stops me and whispers in my ear. "Be careful, okay? You don't really know this man. He's funny and good looking, but you're pretty vulnerable right now. Don't give up your freedom too easily. You worked hard for it."

I nod at her and feel a small flicker of doubt.

At the end of the meal, Vicky suggests we go to a local bar for drinks. We hear the beat of the music as we get out of the car. Over drinks, we listen to the band and try to talk over the noise in the bar. The band starts playing a Jim Reeves song.

Dwayne leans over the table, so I can hear him. "Will you dance with me? I want to teach you the Texas two-step."

I haven't danced since my high school prom, but I say yes. I put my hand in his and follow him. We push our way onto the crowded dance floor. He pulls me close to him and wraps his arm around my waist. He rests his hand on my hip. "Step back with your left foot. Step. Step. Slide."

As I step my left foot back, his right leg moves between my knees. He leans his cheek against mine and sings into my ear, "Put your sweet lips a little closer to the phone." His breath gently stirs my hair, and his mustache bristles against my cheek. We sway our way around the dim dance floor. The pulsing music echoes in my ear. I press my cheek into the curve of his neck with his hand resting against my back.

Too soon we leave the bar. Tod reminds Dwayne he has to get up at four in the morning to drive to Cleveland. We pull into the Chili's parking lot. Vicky has planned for them to drop me off there to pick up my car. They can then take Dwayne to his hotel. She wanted to spare me an uncomfortable conversation about who takes a strange man to a hotel. Finally, Tod stops the car by mine.

Dwayne looks at me in the dim light and grips my hand. "I guess we've got to say goodbye."

Suddenly, I shove him with my shoulder toward the car door. I tell Vicky I will drive Dwayne to his hotel. She swivels around in the front seat to stare at me. She lays her hand on the back of her seat and starts to speak. I glide across the back seat before she can.

By this time, Dwayne has the door open, and he's helping me out of the back seat. We get in my car, and I speed out of the parking lot. At the first stop light, he leans over and gently places his hand against the back of my head. His wide fingers thread through my hair. He pulls me to him. We kiss stretched across the gear shift. Cars honk loudly, and we break apart.

At the hotel outside his room we sit in the dark car without speaking. Then I open the car door and walk to his room. Under the glow of the light over the door, I stand waiting. He joins me there. I take the key card from his hand and open the door. We step into the dark room together.

I sit on the edge of the bed, and he drops down beside me.

The bed sinks with our weight. He lays his arm around my shoulder and pulls me closer to him. I kick off my shoes, and he slides off his boots.

We swivel in unison and fall back against the pillows. He kisses my ear, my nose, my throat, and finally, my mouth. We lie face-to-face in the middle of the bed. I lay my arm over him. I tug his shirt out of his jeans and push my hand up it. I feel the hard, smooth muscles of his back.

He rolls on top of me, and I feel his weight against me. I feel his hand cup my breast. My ragged breath moans from me. I force back the reminder in my head that I've never been with a man except Tom. I have never understood my divorced friends' stories of one-night stands. Now I do.

He jerks away. I look at his face in the glow of the neon light outside the window. He leans on his elbow by my pillow. He pushes my hair gently from my face and kisses the tip of my nose.

I move away from him, trying to sit up. I swing my legs to get out of the bed in an effort to leave the motel room. My face burns with embarrassment.

"Baby, listen." He reaches up and pulls me down by him until I settle into his shoulder. His low voice murmurs in my ear, "I know you'll think I'm crazy. But I can't go through with this. You ain't no one-night stand."

I whisper an apology against his chest. I stumble over the words to say I'm sorry for not being what he wanted. "My God, how could I think anyone would want someone like me?"

He tilts my chin up. We look into each other's eyes. "You are who I want. I just know that the first time we make love is going to be when we have time to enjoy every minute of it and not worry about a damn alarm going off in a couple of hours."

He pauses and strokes the curve of my throat. "I want you to believe me when I say we're going to have the rest of our lives to love each other. I just know I'm going to love you until I die." He laughs softly and murmurs, "After two nasty divorces, I probably shouldn't be such a damn romantic fool."

I tell him about my leaving a brutal marriage and going through a messy divorce myself. "I have never believed in romance, but now I do." I'm not sure if I'm trying to convince him or myself.

As we lie in the darkness together, he tells me about his time as a member of a band in Texas. He wishes he had his guitar here. "We have a song now, you know?"

"We do?"

He sings softly in reply, "I'm a believer." He murmurs the lyrics about finding love at first sight until I relax into his arms.

As I listen to his voice rumbling beneath my ear, I fall asleep. At four in the morning, the alarm wakes us up. Dwayne walks me to my car and kisses me goodbye. I drive home to my sleeping daughter.

Four days later, a letter arrives in the mail. The return address says, *Lonesome Dwayne, Parkview Motel, Cleveland, Ohio.* On the back flap of the envelope, he has drawn a detailed sketch of a lioness from the Cleveland Zoo. Underneath he has written, *Love me back it will be good for you.*

BROKEN PROMISES

After finishing his work at the Cleveland Zoo, Dwayne stops in Springfield, and I climb into the truck to join him on his trip home to Texas. During the weeks after our blind date, we talked each night on the phone and wrote each other a stream of letters. Now as the sun rises behind us, we talk as if we've known each other for years, not as if we just met on a blind date.

After an hour of traveling and sharing stories, he cracks the window and holds a cigarette up. The smoke blows into the wind. He stares at the pavement. "I was in Vietnam right after I turned twenty. I stopped in Bryan to visit my mom after riding a Harley all over the country. A draft notice was waiting for me."

I slide closer to him on the seat, sitting thigh to thigh on the warm vinyl. I lay my hand on his knee.

"It was the only time my master sergeant father was proud of me. I don't like to talk about it but felt I could tell you." He snaps the cigarette out the window. " I don't sleep too good at night sometimes."

"You can tell me anything." I lean against his shoulder.

We stop for gas in Arkansas. Dwayne buys a burrito drying

under the heat lamp and piles jalapeños on it. I buy a piece of fried chicken. Sitting by each other at a scarred wooden picnic table, we eat together, the two of us—the only other time we shared a meal was with Vicky and Tod after they arranged our meeting.

We pull into his driveway in Bryan at sunset. He carries my suitcase into the rusty trailer and down the long narrow hallway. I follow him. We stand by his bed.

Dwayne says, "We've been waiting since our Chili's date for this moment. Do you want to go get some dinner first?"

"I don't want to wait anymore." We move toward each other.

I wake in the night to the sound of the air conditioner rattling in the window. I listen to Dwayne breathing beside me. I stare into the darkness and match my breath to his until I fall asleep.

Over the next three days, Dwayne and I drive across the flat Texas prairies to his mother's house in a small nearby town, and he introduces me to her and his brother, Doug. The small house they share sits in the shadows of live oak trees with a Texas A&M University flag snapping in the wind. We share Sunday dinner together, and his mother, Roberta, tells me stories about Dwayne as a little boy.

On the way home, we pick up his daughter, Jessica, at her mom's house. Dwayne introduces me to Janice, his second wife, and tells her, "I had to go to Missouri to find the perfect woman."

The three of us go to a movie together. Dwayne sits between us and holds both of our hands.

He takes me to Baker's Garage, where he works when he's between jobs. I meet some of his mechanic friends and shake their hands.

He tells them, "This is the girl I'm going to marry."

A month after coming home from my visit, I wait one night for hours for Dwayne's call. I worry about what might have happened to him, and I don't sleep, staring at the ceiling in the dark. My newfound belief in love at first sight fades in the dim light.

The phone rings at six the next morning. He starts talking as soon as I say hello. "I got laid off yesterday. I'm back at Baker's Garage. Call you when I can."

The hum on the line tells me he hung up. I sit, unable to move, at the kitchen table with the phone still in my hand. Minutes click by on the digital clock over the stove until I finally hang it up.

I call him every day, but he never answers or calls back. On my birthday, a florist arrives at my school and brings me a dozen yellow roses. Only his name is written on the card. The roses propel me to make the decision to confront him about his cutting me out of his life. I buy a ticket for a one-day visit to Bryan.

Now the small plane drops out of the Texas sky onto the tarmac with a bump. I rise from the seat, bending my head under the low ceiling. I grip the back of the seat with my shaky hands. I drag my wobbly wheeled suitcase to the door and down the stairs into the blast of the July sun. I blink in the bright sun. My eyes water, and I'm not sure if it's tears or the glare.

Within minutes I am in a rental car and driving through the unfamiliar streets of Bryan. I didn't see much of the town during my short visit. Browning leaves on the few short trees shrivel in the heat. Every street sign lets you know what state you're in. Lone Star Avenue. George Bush Drive. Crockett Street. The Lone Star flag droops in the humid air from flagpoles on most of the lawns.

Soon I pull into the driveway of Baker's Garage. The concrete walls of the building are covered in graffiti, and inside auto parts posters with girls in bikinis hang over the workbenches. All of the garage doors are wide open to catch any cooling breeze.

I recognize Dwayne's scrawny body in faded Wranglers bending over the engine of a truck. I sit in the hot car and practice what I'll say to him. Then I get out of the car and slam the door.

He pulls his head out from under the hood and rubs his hands against the sides of his ragged jeans, smearing grease on them. He takes a step toward me, stopping to stare at me. I lean on the car, feeling the heat of the metal against me.

I watch him without speaking. The other two mechanics look at Dwayne and then me. They stand without moving to watch us.

Dwayne walks toward me and wipes the sweat off his face with a shop towel. "Mary." Only one word as we stare at each other.

I move my gaze over his shoulder to break the eye contact. "We need to talk."

He steps away from me. "Yeah, we do." He waves at his friends and gets into my car. I drive us to the nearby café, the Kettle, where we ate with Jessica.

Beside me, I hear him ask, "How's Steph?" I tell him she's looking forward to her junior year at a private high school.

I ask him about Jessica, who's starting junior high in the fall. He tells me she's nervous but has asked if I'll help her with her English class. The comment halts the conversation. The strain between us hangs in the air. We know we're not talking about the reason for my visit.

When we get to the café, he swings open the door for me and then follows me. In the chill of the air conditioning, I shiver. The waitress leads us to a booth in the back. We order iced tea and sit without speaking or looking at each other until it is delivered.

Dwayne leans across the table to face me. "This only makes it harder, you know."

I dig my fingernails into my palm. "Nothing makes this harder than it already is."

"You need to move on with your life."

After not being able to talk, a flood of words rushes out of me. "I need to know what is going to happen with us. You call me in the middle of the night to tell me you've been laid off your job. Roses show up, yet you've not returned a single damn phone call or answered one letter. I deserve better from someone who claimed he loved me." I close my eyes against a wave of nausea and lean back against the sticky plastic of the seat.

"Exactly. You deserve better. Better than a half-assed mechanic who doesn't have a real job. Better than living in a trashed-out trailer." His voice rises with each word. "Mary, you need to get out of here and get away from me."

He spreads both hands flat on the tabletop. I look at his large capable hands and swallow against the heavy lump in my throat.

"Mary, Mary, Mary," he chants like a prayer. "What the hell are we going to do?"

"That's up to you. You're not including me in the decision."

"Yeah, I'm an asshole. Hate me. Forget me." He stands up abruptly. "I'll walk back to the garage." He turns to leave but pivots to face me.

I bend my head back and look up at him as he stands stiffly above me. I remember Tom standing above me with a face filled with anger. With a deep breath, I stand up, so we are face-to-face.

"Just go home. Find someone who'll make you happy. Don't turn into some psycho jilted woman chasing me around. This is over." He marches away. I watch his familiar stride until he goes out the door. He doesn't turn around.

I sit in the café through the hours until my plane leaves. I drink one glass of iced tea after another brought by the sympathetic waitress. She asks if I need a menu, and I tell her I'm not hungry. Somewhere about the fifth glass of tea, she pats my hand. "Men are full of shit, girl."

When it gets close to time for my flight, I get into my rental car and drive back to the airport. I take the midnight flight home.

I focus on being a teacher and on being a mother. I teach drama to my summer school students, and I pretend to laugh at their jokes. Stephanie and I take our summer trip to Kansas City and shop for clothes for the upcoming school year. For the first time, I don't enjoy shopping with her.

The summer passes in a blur. My divorce becomes final. I drink too much wine. I sleep too little. I lose thirty pounds.

I don't believe in love anymore. Every year I teach *Romeo and Juliet* to my freshmen students. The adolescent girls in my class obsess over the story of doomed passion and are always searching for their one true love. Their soulmate. They cry on my shoulder when a boy doesn't change into their Romeo. I always tell them they can't depend upon a man to save them.

Now the lesson I teach the girls becomes a bitter pill of truth. Love at first sight is a myth. A Romeo and Juliet lie.

September for a teacher always promises a new start. After the beginning of school, I pack a small box with the gifts Dwayne gave me in our few weeks together. A Harley T-shirt. A pair of silver earrings. A book of the paintings by his favorite artist, Salvador Dali. A small stack of the sketches he drew for me.

Next, I put in the packet of his letters tied with a blue ribbon. I can tell the order they're written by the return addresses. *Lonesome Dwayne. Falling in Love Dwayne. Missing You Dwayne. The Man Who Can't Live Without You.*

Finally, I write and place a final letter to him on top. We got to know each other through those first letters after our blind date. Now I have tried to put my feelings into a few words. *I miss you. I still love you. Your Mary.*

I mail the box to Dwayne. I have no expectation of an answer.

Four weeks pass. I'm fixing dinner when Stephanie slams into the apartment after school. She skids the mail onto the counter by me. A corner of an envelope sticks out of the pile. I recognize the writing. The return address only has his name. Dwayne.

I flee to the bathroom with the envelope. I slip down the wall and sit with my back against the cool porcelain of the bathtub. The letter is short. *Getting my gifts back broke what was left of my heart. I miss the sound of your voice through the phone. I won't ask you to forget what I did. Can you forgive me? Call me. D*

But I don't call. I carry the letter around with me and read it several times a day. The paper wrinkles and creases. The ink smears on the envelope. I wake each morning to the same question. Can I ever trust him?

After two weeks of agonizing over the letter, I reach for the phone. Sitting in the middle of my tangled sheets after another sleepless night, I grip the phone in my sweaty hand.

He picks up on the second ring and says hello. There's his familiar twang.

"It's me," I say in a shaky voice.

"Mary. Baby." His name for me fills the distance between us.

After talking about our daughters and his work at the garage rebuilding cars, we agree to be more cautious this time. Before saying goodbye, Dwayne says, "You are my best friend. Let's be that for now. I'm a lousy husband."

I tell him I would love for us to spend time together as friends.

Both of us may be too afraid to be more than friends, but every three weeks, one of us drives the six hundred miles between Texas and Missouri for short visits. We leave each other each night and sleep in motel rooms.

I learn to cover my ears when the drag cars blast across the starting line. He wears his starched Wranglers and cowboy boots to my students' plays and to chaperone the homecoming dance with me.

By November, he gets back his job at the research equipment company. He's on the road all the time now. We end most nights talking on the phone. During one call, he complains about the assistants his company sends him. "They can't follow a simple instruction on how to do something without arguing with me."

I laugh and tell him I was my dad's assistant carpenter. "He taught me to keep quiet and to do what he told me."

Dwayne doesn't say anything for a few seconds. "How would you like to be my assistant on weekends and on your breaks?"

I don't hesitate. "I would love that."

"I'm going to teach you how to build gorilla cages and lab cubicles. What do you think about that?"

"I can't wait."

As Dwayne's assistant, I fly into the place where he is working. Baltimore. Long Island. Mississippi. I walk off airplanes and find him waiting for me. His tanned mustached face wrinkles into a grin when I wave across the crowd. As we work side by side, I do learn to build laboratory cubicles and zoo equipment. We become better friends and now coworkers, but we still sleep in separate hotel rooms.

In each city, we always visit a Harley-Davidson dealer. We buy T-shirts, and Dwayne draws a crowd with his stories of motorcycle rallies and kick-start Harleys. He walks around the gleaming motorcycles and describes each one. I soon can match the cryptic Harley code letters to the bike. FLHT are baggers. FLSTC are Heritage Classics. FXDF are Fat Bobs. I watch women riders with envy when they wheel their Harleys into the dealership parking lots.

Often I follow Dwayne into the back area where the mechanics work on the motorcycles. He and one of them lean over a Harley with its engine parts scattered on the floor and talk about how to make it run faster. I begin to feel at home there in the brightly lit space with the sound of the powerful motors booming off the walls.

On a visit to Bob Dron Harley in Oakland, we stand face-to-face across a shiny candy-apple-red Harley, a Fat Boy model. Its chrome V-twin motor and low-slung body stretch close to the ground and promise speed and adventure.

Simultaneously, we sigh our appreciation for the bike in a long *aaaah*. Dwayne grins at me. "You really would ride a Harley with me?"

I laugh out loud. "You promised me on our blind date you'd take me for a ride. I'm still waiting." Across the black leather seat, I reach out and grab his hand.

We drive back to the airport and board separate planes home. I know my students will want to know about my adventures the next morning. I lean my head against the cool window and drift off to sleep. I dream of flying—on two wheels. I feel the vibration of the engine under me on my own motorcycle. Independent. Free.

Many nights at home, I fall asleep with a phone tucked against my ear with his voice on the other end. Often he plays his guitar and sings to me across the miles. One midnight I whisper, "I love you."

He whispers back, "I love you too." We both hold our breath for a moment.

One week later on a sunny afternoon in Los Angeles, he picks me up at LAX, and we walk into our motel's lobby. Dwayne takes the handle of my suitcase and shows me a single room key card.

I take one end of it while he holds the other. He touches my cheek. "This time we're sharing a room." It's not a question.

I lay my hand on his shoulder. I pull him close and tiptoe up to reach his lips.

We walk to the elevator. I open the door of our room for us the way I did on the night of our blind date. Later that night we fall asleep together for the first time since he left me with a glass of tea in a Bryan café.

SNOW

Dwayne calls me from Love's Truck Stop in Oklahoma. "Baby, Jessica and me are halfway to Missouri. We'll be there in about four hours."

"The turkey will be ready by then." I stop and listen to the roar of trucks behind him. "I just hope Jessica and Stephanie get along okay." We both know that the family of four sitting around the Thanksgiving dinner table will include Stephanie and Jessica, our two teenage girls who've never met.

"Everything's going to be okay, I promise. Our girls just want us to be happy." He clicks his lighter, and I can see him there leaning against the wall with the cigarette dangling in his fingers.

I go back to the kitchen to continue cooking our holiday meal. I pop open the oven and squeeze broth over the browning turkey. I mix the ingredients for Millionaire's Pies. It wouldn't be Thanksgiving without my mom's trademark pies.

As I move around the kitchen putting together the meal, I think about what's happened in my life over the last year. From a blind date to a breakup to a Thanksgiving dinner with our daughters.

I left a message on Steven's phone this morning wishing him

a happy Thanksgiving and inviting him to join us. He won't call me back. We haven't spoken since the divorce became final. He's also ignored Mom's invitation.

I perch on a stool at the kitchen counter and check my watch. This morning Stephanie has insisted on going to a friend's house even if it is Thanksgiving. She should be home in a couple of hours, before Dwayne and Jessica arrive. A knot of nervousness ties in my stomach. Each daughter has accepted a new person in her parent's life, but now they have to like each other.

I'm sliding the turkey out of the oven when I hear Dwayne's truck pull into the driveway. The engine dies with a cough and a sputter. The last time he visited me, the heater stopped working, and he drove the six hundred miles with his jacket stuffed into the vent to keep out the freezing air.

I run to the front door and swing it open. I stand on the small front porch and watch the two of them step out of the truck. The man I love and his daughter—who may one day be my stepdaughter. Dwayne reaches into the bed of the battered Chevy truck and pulls out their suitcases. I wrap my sweater more tightly around me against the chilly winter air.

Dropping the suitcases, Dwayne leaps up onto the top step by me and sweeps me into a hug. Behind him, I see Jessica stop by the bottom step. She shivers in the cold in her thin T-shirt without a jacket. Her white blond hair lifts in the brisk wind. She chews on her bottom lip as she watches her father and me.

"Jessica, let's get you in the house where it's warm." She smiles at me and comes up the steps. I hug her, and for a moment, she stands still. She wraps her arms around my waist and hugs me back.

"Is it always like this in November?"

"Yeah, it's that time of the year. Pretty typical for this part of Missouri."

"I've never seen snow. Daddy told me we had snow once in Bryan, but I was just a baby."

Once we get in the house, I tell Jessica she'll be staying in Stephanie's room in the extra bed. We watch Dwayne carry the suitcases up the stairs. He drops hers in Stephanie's room. He walks down the short hallway to my room and stops at the top of the stairs. He looks down the stairs at the two of us standing there.

Dwayne opens my bedroom door and drops his suitcase inside the room. Until he comes back down the stairs, Jessica and I don't talk or look at each other as we watch him.

"Something sure smells good in here, baby." Dwayne takes my hand.

"I think dinner is about ready. I'm just waiting for Stephanie to get home. Come on in the kitchen, and you can have a piece of fresh warm bread until she gets here." I place my hand on Jessica's shoulder and guide her across the living room into the kitchen.

I put out the butter and a jar of my mom's blackberry preserves and pile fresh rolls into a basket.

Jessica juggles a hot roll onto a plate. "You made these?"

"Don't think I do this all the time. But it wouldn't be Thanksgiving without homemade bread in my house."

"My mom doesn't cook much. I usually order pizza, or she brings home food from Sonic." She smears butter and jelly on a roll and pops it in her mouth.

Dwayne watches her and laughs. "I told you she was a good cook. This scrawny redneck's going to get fat."

The three of us stand there leaning across the kitchen counter and eating the fragrant bread, butter dripping off our fingers. The quiet is broken by the sound of the garage door squealing open. The thin walls between the kitchen and the garage vibrate with the thumping bass. Pink Floyd.

"Stephanie's home." I walk to the door leading to the garage and open it. Dwayne and Jessica follow me. We stand in the doorway and watch her in the small blue car with the Grateful Dead stickers. The music dies as she turns it off. She eases open the door to avoid banging into my car. She joins us at the door.

"I know I'm late, but Heather and I wanted to listen to a new CD." She pulls off her knit cap, and her hair frizzes in the cold air.

I take her hand and kiss her on the forehead. The faintest whiff of marijuana smoke lingers on her clothes. I am aware of Dwayne and Jessica behind me, so I keep quiet.

Dwayne moves to stand beside me and puts his arm over Jessica's shoulder. "Steph, this is Jessica."

Stephanie and Jessica stand and look at each other. None of us talk.

Then Stephanie smiles at her. "Let's go up to my room. We'll unpack your stuff. What kind of music do you like?"

They walk away from us, and I don't hear Jessica's reply. I lean forward and rest my forehead against Dwayne's solid chest.

He places his callused hand on my head and strokes my hair. "That wasn't so bad, was it?"

"Maybe it'll be okay after all." I worry quietly.

I rush to put dinner on the table. Dwayne drinks coffee and talks while I'm working. Mashing potatoes. Pulling the green-bean casserole out of the oven. Setting bowls of food on the table.

Dwayne's stories fill the warm space. He waves his hands in the air as he describes the time Jessica rode her tricycle, eating a hot dog. "She fell off the porch and landed hot dog up." He adds he knew then she'd be a hell of a motorcycle rider.

Each time I pass him, one of us reaches out and touches the other. A hand on the shoulder. Fingertips to fingertips. My hand on his knee. We agreed we don't want to make the girls uncomfortable, but we can't be in the same room without touching. Magnets drawn to each other.

I yell up the stairs that dinner's ready. The blast of the music can be heard through the closed door. I shout again.

The door opens, and our two girls come out laughing. They walk side by side down the stairs. I smile at the sight of them. Stephanie has French braided Jessica's hair, and she wears one of Stephanie's Grateful Dead T-shirts.

Dwayne and I sit across from each other with our daughters between us. He carves the turkey. We pass around the bowls filled with steaming food. We laugh at Dwayne's story of the Thanksgiving when he and his brother, Doug, won the washer-tossing contest. They had their pictures taken with the Bud Light girls. When the picture was printed in the newspaper, Dwayne's hair, blowing in the wind, made him look as if he had horns. "A Texas longhorn." He laughs.

Stephanie tells the story of the time I dropped a pie as I was taking it out of the oven. "I swear to God, she caught the pan. The pie twirled in the air and fell back in the pan. It was scrambled but not on the floor."

"It was your favorite pie. I couldn't lose it. You ate it with a spoon, right out of the pan."

I scoot my chair over by her and pull her close to me. "I love you, sweetie."

She rolls her eyes. "Love you too, Mom." I move my chair back to my plate.

Jessica stiffens in her chair and stares at me and Stephanie. Her hand trembles against the table. "My mom tells me her life was ruined the day I was born."

I struggle to find the right words to say. I know from years of dealing with young girls that their trusting you with a big secret requires a careful response to show you care and don't dismiss their pain.

Before I can speak, Dwayne says, "You made my life worth living." He gets out of his chair and kneels by hers and wraps his arms around her. She leans against his shoulder for a minute. He wipes her tears with a napkin.

I reach across the table and lay my hand on Jessica's, rubbing it gently. We sit like that for a few minutes.

Then we all start eating again. Forks clink against the plates. Dwayne asks the girls about school.

The wind rattles the glass patio doors by the table. We stop talking and look at the trees whipping back and forth. Pellets of sleet crackle against the windows and the door.

Jessica puts down her fork. "Do you think it will snow?"

"It may stay ice, or it may switch to snow. Depends on the temperature." I start stacking plates.

"Let me help." Jessica takes them from my hand.

"Thanks."

Stephanie and Dwayne get up to help us. Jessica tells them she'll clean up with me. She turns to me and asks if that's okay.

"I am sure Stephanie will not miss doing the dishes."

Dwayne and Stephanie go into the living room to watch TV. In a few minutes, I can hear the Loony Tunes theme music.

"Daddy loves those cartoons! He always makes me laugh with his Elmer Fudd imitation."

"Me too."

We work together to tidy the kitchen and start the dishwasher. Every few minutes, Jessica presses her face against the glass door and watches for the first snowflake to fall. Nothing yet. Then she goes back to helping me.

When we're done, we go to the living room to watch TV with Dwayne and Stephanie. The four of us sit together on the couch, our bodies squashed together, Dwayne and I on each end with the girls between us. Our fingers touch behind their backs.

After we finish watching the cartoons, Dwayne gets up to go outside to smoke. I remind him it's freezing outside.

"Smokers are like mailmen. Neither hail nor sleet nor snow can stop us from smoking that cigarette."

I hear the patio door close in the next room, and I go back to watching TV. Then the door bangs open, the vertical blinds clinking in the wind.

Dwayne runs into the room and shouts, "Jessie Lane, it is fucking snowing outside!"

Jessica leaps off the couch, and the two of them run out the open door. Stephanie and I stand up and look at each other.

"Mom, are they seriously that excited about snow?"

"I think this may be a Texas thing. Let's go join them." We take the time to put on shoes and coats before going outside.

We walk out the door to find Dwayne and Jessica standing in the middle of the frozen brown grass. Their faces turn up at the sky with their mouths open. Fat snowflakes swirl around them. A few fall into their mouths.

Stephanie and I stop for a minute, just looking at them. Then we join them. We link our hands and form a circle. The icy crystals sting our skin. At some point, we begin to dance in a circle, shuffling and kicking around and around on the cracking dead leaves beneath our feet.

Dwayne laughs and tells me, "We're a family now, Mary Jane."

Stephanie's hand slides out of mine. I turn and look at her. She crosses her arms across her chest and moves away from us.

I drop Dwayne's hand and walk to my daughter. I grab both of her hands and pull her to me. Cheek to cheek, warm in the cold. Snowflakes melt in our hair. "You and me, Stephanie Lynn. We'll always be together. You're my family no matter what."

AN ATTACK
OF THE HEART

A s I shove my key in the front door, I can hear the shrill ringing of the phone, and it seems to signal bad news. I push the door open quickly, banging it into the wall behind it. I drop my purse on the floor. I sprint to grab it before it stops ringing even though I know Dwayne isn't supposed to call until later. I act out of a need to hear his voice. *He should still be at work in Texas*, I remind myself.

Our conversation last night was a tense one, and I think he might be calling to see if I'm okay. Since our Thanksgiving with both daughters, we've been trying to figure out who is going to move their daughter to another state.

Dwayne treats Stephanie as if she were his daughter. He buys her gifts the way Tom never did, and he talks to her each night when he calls to find out how she is. He slips her a twenty when he visits, so she has gas money.

But we struggle to get past my resistance to getting married again. I want to spend every day with him, but the idea of being married again scares me. After my first wedding, I was trapped for twenty-three years. I know he is not Tom, but the fear remains. "Can't we live in sin?" I ask him.

Dwayne refuses to move me to Texas without being married. "I'm not moving the woman I love with her teenage daughter to another state without our being married."

I pick up the phone on the fourth ring. I answer it with a breathless hello from the rush to the phone.

"Mary, Dwayne's had a heart attack," a voice shouts in my ear. Both the news and the fact that the voice belongs to Janice, his second wife and Jessica's mother, shocks me into silence for a moment.

I finally find my voice and ask her how he is. She tells me a coworker found him slumped in the sanding booth at his work. He called 911, and now Dwayne remains in the emergency room. She pauses and tells me he's been unconscious since the ambulance brought him to the emergency room.

I hear her take a deep breath. "It's a small town. They know I'm his ex-wife and his daughter's mother, so they called me. I grabbed Jessica and got here as fast as I could. That's when they told me he asked the co-worker who found him for Mary." We hear the wires thrumming as the silence stretches between us.

I tell her I'll be there as soon as I can. It's an eight-hour drive to Bryan, I remind her. She gives me the phone number of the waiting room. As soon as I hang up, I quickly pack a suitcase and wait for Stephanie to get home from school. Then I take her to my mom's house to stay until I return. I begin my long trip to Texas.

The sky darkens into midnight and lightens into dawn as I drive south. The tires rumble against the pavement. I push the radio buttons repeatedly during the hours and listen to a static-filled stream of old country music and preachers' sermons. My eyes burn from tears and exhaustion. A headache thumps behind my temples.

I stop at a truck stop in the middle of Oklahoma. I lean against a grimy wall by the pay phone and call the hospital waiting room. I listen to the ringing across the miles.

Jessica answers and tells me her father has been in and out of tests all day. Her voice cracks as she whispers that he still isn't awake. "Are you going to be here soon?"

I promise her I'll be there as soon as I can. I set the receiver down gently. I lay my forehead against the cold plastic. Then I walk outside and continue my journey.

The sun is rising in a blaze of orange and red behind the parking lot when I arrive at the hospital. I slam the car door behind me and follow the red signs leading to the main entrance and step through the sliding doors to see an elderly woman with soft curled white hair sitting at the entrance desk.

"Good morning, dear!" She leans forward to greet me. I ask her for Dwayne's room number. As she thumbs through the register book, she asks if I'm a family member. I hesitate as I consider my answer. She raises her head to look at me.

"I'm going to be his wife." She raises her penciled eyebrows at my answer and gives me the room number.

I walk down a maze of lime-green hallways until I find the room number. When I push open the door, I understand the raised eyebrows of the greeter. Standing on each side of the bed are Janice and Kathy, both of his former wives. In a corner of the room Jessica is curled up in a chair.

Dwayne lies in the middle of the stiff white sheets in the bed. His chest rises and falls with his measured, steady breaths while a machine beeps rhythmically in the corner. I move to stand at the foot of the bed. Both women turn to look at me. After a few minutes, Kathy moves away from the bed and leans against the closed door.

I walk to the now empty side of the bed. Across his quiet form, I ask Janice if he's talked to anyone. She shakes her head no and tells me the doctor thinks he's aware of what's going on; the medicine is keeping him asleep for now.

I perch on the side of the bed and rest my hand on his unmoving hands resting on his chest. I watch him while his heart beats tick up and down on the EKG monitor. All of us in the room remain motionless in our places for what seems to be an unbearably long time.

Finally, I watch his eyelids flutter and open. I lean forward. I whisper in his ear. "I'm here, darlin'."

He grabs my hand between both of his. "It took you long enough," he croaks. He grins at me, and I laugh out loud with relief.

Janice backs away from the bed. Jessica gets up and sits across from me. "Daddy, I was worried about you."

He reaches up with one hand and caresses her cheek. "I'm going to be fine, Jessie Lane."

Janice tells her they need to go home and let her father rest. She stops and glances at me. "Mary will take care of your dad." They leave with a promise to visit him soon.

As they walk out the door, I notice that Kathy is gone. She left without a word.

Dwayne asks, "Did I just dream that both Kathy and Janice were here with you?" I smile and say yes.

He laughs. "Damn, that almost gave me another heart attack." I know he's better if he's back to joking about his ex-wives.

Midafternoon the doctors announce it was an angina episode, not a heart attack, probably caused by a virus he caught in a research laboratory somewhere doing his job. Relieved, I take him home. We spend the next few days experiencing waking up together each morning and ending the day as a couple.

Sometimes in the middle of the night, he wakes with a violent lurch and a shout. I hug him and he whispers, "In country again."

I cradle him in my arms until he falls back asleep, hoping Vietnam and the war don't wake him.

After a week, I need to get back to my classroom. My students will be missing me, and it will take days to recover from a substitute teacher. Dwayne returns to winching out a car motor in his garage, so I know he's gotten back his strength.

He takes me to the airport. As the plane rises into the air, I look down at the flat brown land beneath me. "That's my new home," I whisper.

THE PROPOSAL

hree weeks after my return home, I fly into Philadelphia on a bitterly cold January day to help him finish a job at the zoo. We drive through the icy streets on the day after thirty-eight inches of snow have fallen.

The next morning we begin building more protective hibernation cages for polar bears. Zoo workers lead us down a short hallway with concrete block walls to get to the main compound where we'll build the thick-walled enclosures for the bears, creating warm caves for them.

On our right a pair of steel doors with a row of padlocks keeping them locked shakes and rattles. The zoo worker yells over his shoulder, "We put the bears in there until you get the cages built. Make sure you stay to the left. They like to stick their paws under the door."

Dwayne and I press ourselves against the rough concrete wall, away from the doors. A loud roar fills the air. A grimy white paw appears in the gap under the door. The claws dig into the concrete floor. Dwayne reaches back and takes my hand, and we move past the paw as it disappears again.

When we reach the area where we're building the cages, stacks of steel poles and sheets of metal are piled up. They have set up the welder for Dwayne under a makeshift tent with his toolboxes, which were shipped from his company.

We begin to work. I cut the metal with a buzzing saw. Dwayne welds pieces together, the flame blazing in the shadowy light. Out in the icy enclosure, I grip the walls until he taps them tightly into place, drilling the screws into the metal.

By afternoon sleet falls and covers us. My eyelashes freeze shut. Siding off my gloves, I hold my warm hand over them to melt the ice.

Dwayne sends me back to the workroom, saying he will finish the last of the job. "You're a hell of a worker, but I don't want you to get sick."

I grade my students' essays while I wait. Zoo workers come in for coffee and then go back out into the cold. I stop and talk to them as they come and go, and sometimes they share their food.

Finally, Dwayne comes to get me. He strips off his frozen coat and hat. I hand him a paper cup of acrid coffee. He wraps his hands around the hot cup. "Shit, us Texans can't stand this cold."

The door swings open with a bang, and all the workers crowd into the room with us. One man yells at Dwayne, "Hey, you gotta marry this girl! She sat here all afternoon and didn't say a goddamn word."

"Hell, my old lady would have started bitching within thirty minutes," another man shouts at us.

Several voices join the chorus. "Yeah, we like this girl."

"If you don't marry her, I will." Loud laughter fills the room.

Dwayne smiles. He reaches out and takes my hand. "Can you see spending your life with a scrawny Texas redneck? Will you stand in front of a preacher and marry me?"

"Is that a formal proposal?" I shake my head and smile at the unromantic setting and the public decision I'm going to have to make. The workers fall silent.

"I tried to live without you and couldn't do it. I thought I was going to die, and you're all I wanted to see before I did." He pulls me to his chest. I feel his warmth beneath the chilly shirt. "Mary Jane, will you marry me?"

I nod a yes. The workers slap us on the back and congratulate themselves on being such good matchmakers.

Two weeks later I fly to Houston for a visit and to talk to Jessica about marrying her father. Dwayne meets me at the gate with a diamond ring. He slips it on my finger, and as we walk through the terminal to the parking lot, everyone we see yells at us, "Did she say yes?"

He holds up my hand with its new ring and gives them a thumbs-up. "Welcome home to Texas, baby."

A WEDDING VOW
AND A FINAL GOODBYE

We marry on a sunny June day in Eureka Springs, Arkansas. Our minister and wedding photographer owns the Wild Bill Wedding Chapel. Dwayne wears his black Stetson, bolo tie, starched Wranglers, and polished cowboy boots. Our daughters and I dress in saloon girl outfits for our wedding photograph. Dwayne adds a sheriff's badge and a fake six-shooter in a holster to his wardrobe.

We stand outside on the curb after the wedding. A group of Harleys arrive with a loud rumble and roar of pipes. With our hands linked, we watch them push the motorcycles' back tires against the curb in front of us.

Dwayne points to them, waving his cigarette in the air. "God, I miss riding a Harley. It's all that saved me after I got back from Vietnam."

"Let's get one together," I decide for us. We smile at each other.

He holds my left hand with its new wedding ring against his chest. "Joined at the heart."

On our wedding night we play miniature golf and eat pizza

with our daughters. Later we lie side by side in bed for the first time as a married couple, my head fitting into his shoulder.

The sound of an *I Love Lucy* marathon drifts up from downstairs where Stephanie and Jessica are sleeping. We listen to their quiet giggling. They took turns using the Jacuzzi tub in our honeymoon suite.

Dwayne whispers in my ear as I fall asleep, "I've never been a lucky man until now. A wife and two daughters. You're stuck with me now, baby."

"We're going to grow old together." We fall asleep curved into each other.

One week after our wedding Dwayne and I drive a moving truck to Tom's house after he demands I come see him. Since our divorce, we only talk on the phone when we're arguing about Stephanie not visiting him. He hangs up if Dwayne answers the phone. He knows Dwayne and I are a couple. But he doesn't know we are now married.

Yesterday the phone rang as I carried a box to the truck. We were loading it for my move to Texas. I answered it, and without a hello, Tom responded, "Stephanie is supposed to have dinner with me and her brother. Is she going to come?"

"I'll remind her about dinner." Then I forced myself to say, "Tom, I got married last week, and I'm moving to Texas."

His labored breath and raspy throat clearing grated against my ear. "What about Stephanie?"

"She has decided to go with us."

"I won't let that happen."

"The judge told both of us that at seventeen she makes her own decision about where to live."

"You may be his wife now. He won't get my daughter too."

I clutched the phone in my clammy hand and waited for his next demand.

"Get your ass out here to talk to me."

"I won't come to that house."

Then he insisted I bring a piece of his furniture to him before I left town: an old oak washstand of his mother's I refinished years ago. I stared at it against the wall as he reminded me it was his mom's, not mine. One last unreasonable demand, I told myself.

"We will be there at ten tomorrow morning with it." I gripped the receiver. "Then I never want to see you again."

"We? You bitch." He slammed down the phone.

Now Dwayne swings the truck onto the narrow road leading to Tom's house. My stomach knots, and I lean against the sun-warmed window. My hands clench against my thighs.

Dwayne reaches across the truck and lays one gentle hand on my shoulder. I sit up straight on the hard vinyl seat and flinch away from his hand.

"Baby, he can't hurt you anymore." He grabs my hand and laces my fingers through his. "You're like a beat dog with him."

"Thanks to you, I'm not afraid anymore—but I dread seeing him again." I scoot next to him and squeeze his hand in mine.

In front of us the large brick house looms. As Dwayne backs up the truck, I watch the door open. Tom comes out on the front step and stops.

He's wearing a starched shirt and tie, ready to go to work. Every Sunday after church, I would starch and iron those shirts. He's president of the State Employees Credit Union, and one time his connection to the Highway Patrol cut off my escape from him. A patrolman advised me to go home to my husband when I tried to report bruises and sprains.

As Dwayne rolls up the rear door, I watch him walk toward us. He keeps his eyes on me, and I step backward on the hot asphalt. Dwayne glances at me. Then he swivels to face Tom. The two men face each other. Tom looks away first. He glares over Dwayne's shoulder at me.

I move forward and place my hand on Dwayne's arm. "You wanted the washstand. Here it is."

Tom looks at me and points at Dwayne. "He can take it inside. I want to talk to you alone."

Dwayne stiffens. "Take your goddamn washstand off the truck. You aren't talking to my wife."

My wife hangs in the air. Standing side by side, Dwayne and I are immobile in the hot June sun. Tom glares at us.

Finally, Tom goes to the truck and begins to slide the small washstand off the truck. He struggles to lift it down, but neither of us moves to help him. He staggers when he tries to carry it. The back of his blue shirt darkens with sweat.

Dwayne moves to the front door and opens it. Tom maneuvers the stand through the door. Dwayne looks at me. He turns to watch Tom's back as he moves down the hallway. Then he steps inside and closes the front door behind them with a bang.

I drop down on the truck bumper and wonder what's being said on the other side of the heavy wooden door. After a few minutes, Dwayne comes outside. He shuts the door behind him.

I stand up, and he says, "Let's head to Texas."

As he starts the truck, I put one hand on the steering wheel. "What did you say to him?"

"I said what needed to be said." He clicks the truck into gear, and it lurches forward. "He's Stephanie's dad, but he's never going to mess with you again."

We drive to Mom's house to pick up his truck. Stephanie is staying with her and joining us in two weeks. I gave in to her pleading and crying for a few more days with her friends since she won't be with them her senior year.

Mom and Stephanie join us in the driveway to say goodbye.

Dwayne and I take turns hugging each of them before we leave. I hold Stephanie close and whisper in her ear. "I swear I'll do anything I can to give you a real home."

"I've never lived anywhere but here."

I tuck her hair behind her ears and kiss her cheek. For a minute, she leans into me.

"Let's go, baby." Dwayne flips his cigarette butt onto the concrete. "You want to drive the U-Haul or my truck?"

Mom looks at me in surprise. "Mary can't drive that big U-Haul."

"Mary can drive any vehicle. Hell, someday I'm putting her on a Harley."

My eyes swing between the two of them. Then I climb up into the driver's seat of the moving truck. I turn the key, and the engine rumbles to life.

A NEW HOMETOWN
AND A NEW FAMILY

I drive the bulky U-Haul truck south six hundred miles to Bryan, Texas. Springfield, my home for over twenty years, grows smaller in the rearview mirror until it fades from my sight. Around me the familiar mountains smooth into broad grassy fields, tall grass waving in the wind. Night falls somewhere near the Texas state line. The glow of Dwayne's headlights behind me guides me though the darkness. At a truck stop in Dallas, I put gas in the truck, and the heat and humidity blanket me.

Dwayne buys his weekly lottery ticket. He says, "Redneck retirement. I could give you and our girls everything you want with that kind of money."

Finally, at midnight I turn onto Welcome Lane, Dwayne's street. I've always thought it was the perfect name for a street for him. Our lights glare across the yard, and the shabby mobile home stands in the spotlight.

Simultaneously we shut off our truck motors. Dwayne's truck door bangs shut behind him. I swing my door open. In the glow of the yard light, he reaches into the truck and takes both of my hands to help me step out of the truck. Hand in hand we walk across the patchy brown grass and the wooden deck to the front door. He sticks the key in the lock and swings open the front door. But he puts a hand on my elbow and stops me from walking through it.

With one arm across my shoulders and one behind my knees, he sweeps me into his arms and cradles me against his chest. His laugh rumbles in his chest against my ear. "I'm going to start this marriage right."

In his arms, I enter my new home. I've been here before on visits. We first made love here. But it feels different now that I am his wife. Now this is my home. My daughter's home.

Dwayne eases me down, and I look around the living room with its sagging plaid couch and the small kitchen with the chipped refrigerator. He tells me he'll get us a couple of glasses of iced tea.

As he clinks ice cubes into glasses, I tell him I'll call Stephanie. After ringing several times, she answers the phone with a sleep-filled voice. "Hi, sweetie, just wanted to tell you Dwayne and I made it. Can't wait for you to join us."

Silence stretches between us. "I miss you, Mom."

"Miss you too." I tell her to go back to sleep. I join Dwayne in the bedroom and stand in the doorway, watching him sip tea and flip through a hot rod magazine.

He looks up at me. "Which side of the bed do you want?" Since the bedroom is so narrow, one side is against the wall. Whoever sleeps there will need to crawl over the other person to get out of bed.

"I'll take the wall side." I strip off my clothes. Dwayne stands up and folds back the blankets. Throwing off his clothes, he joins me. My head slips into the nook of his shoulder.

I open my eyes to sunshine streaming through the window. Sitting up suddenly, I check the time on the clock beside the bed.

Eight in the morning. I press my hand against my chest with its pounding heart, filled with an unreasonable sense of panic. I can't remember the last time I slept through the night without waking. For years, I would be startled awake by Tom's fist pounding into the pillow by my head. He never hit me, just propelled me from sleep to consciousness in seconds. As I quivered there with my heart pounding, he'd whisper all of the things I'd done to make him mad. The attacks were random. But now I always sleep with a part of me waiting for an assault.

On this sunny Texas morning, I take a deep breath. *Safe. I'm safe here.* In the kitchen, I hear Dwayne singing and smell the coffee brewing.

Soon he comes into the room with cups in his hands. "How's my wife doing this morning?"

"I never woke up once." I wrap my hand around the heat of the mug.

"Yeah, no nightmares for me either."

Dwayne sits by me and leans against the headboard, holding his coffee with one hand and stroking my bare arm with the other. I stretch my legs out by his, feeling his warmth beside me, and listen to his story of talking the woman who owned the property into letting him move here without money up front.

"I was homeless and divorced. I had to declare bankruptcy after Janice ran up the credit cards. Lost my business." He describes how he drove around until he found this abandoned trailer. "It had a hell of a garage though."

Now it is our home. And Stephanie will be coming here in a few days.

Dwayne stands up. "What do you want to do today, baby?"

I climb out of bed and dig through my suitcase on the floor. "We've got to unpack some of my stuff, and then I'd like to go to your bank and get our account set up."

When he doesn't answer, I stop dressing and look at him.

He plops down on the bed. "I haven't had a bank account since the bankruptcy. I pay for everything with cash and money orders." He reaches over and opens a dresser drawer. He pulls out a large manila envelope and hands it to me. "My bank."

I open it and look at the cash stuffed inside it.

He lays one large scarred hand on my knee. "I'm making good money at REC right now. I promise I'll take care of you and Steph."

We sit side by side on the edge of our small bed. I rub his shoulder under his Harley T-shirt. The air conditioner rumbles, and cool air lifts my hair.

"How about I have a bank account? Soon I'll have the money from the house Tom and I are selling." I tell him I'll have paychecks again when I get a teaching job. "You keep paying cash for things."

He smiles. "Make it a joint account. REC pays me in cash, so I can put some in the bank for us."

After breakfast, we drive into town. Dwayne points out the building where he had his custom motorcycle shop after he got back from Vietnam. We walk out of the bank thirty minutes later with a joint account. We sit in the truck in the parking lot, with me holding our new checkbook.

Dwayne starts the engine and turns on the air conditioner. He cracks the window and lights a cigarette. He takes my hand. "All I got is yours now."

I smile at him. "Same here." Then I shove the checkbook into the glove box.

Dwayne throws the cigarette out the window. "Let's make a deal. Any money we have is ours. You buy what you want. I buy what I want."

I nod in agreement. "No asking. No permission. Partners."

We shake hands on the deal. Dwayne says, "You don't need me to let you do anything."

"I've never been married like that."

"Me either, baby."

Over the next two weeks, we spend the days trying to find a house for our new family. The down payment for it will be provided by my share of the house Tom and I owned together.

As we drive through the streets and roads of the neighboring towns of Bryan and College Station, I become familiar with the people and the landscape.

Twisted trees thrust up through the concrete-like caliche soil. The edge of the land extends for miles out to the distant horizon under the cathedral arch of the pale blue sky. Massive trucks known as duallies with muddy double back tires belch smoke from their diesel engines.

The men in starched Wrangler jeans and cowboy boots wear their summer straw cowboy hats. All of them, like Dwayne, tuck their pearl-snap shirts or T-shirts into their jeans with a thick leather belt adorned with a substantial buckle.

The women stroll through the hot days with their hair sprayed stiff, so it remains unmoved by the humidity or gusts of wind. Thin, light summer dresses in a garden of floral prints sway as they walk. They wear elaborately decorated cowboy boots with the dresses when they go dancing. Their faces remain perfectly made-up with arched penciled eyebrows and bright lipstick.

In an hour, my makeup melts off my face. In the steamy heat my hair frizzes. But my closet fills with the cool flowing dresses. My warm Missouri clothes remain packed. Dwayne buys me my first pair of cowboy boots.

Each night I sleep content, tucked between the wood-paneled walls and the warmth of Dwayne's solid body.

Every day I call Stephanie. Sometimes two or three times a

day. I hear the nervousness in her voice. I try to cheer her up with stories about Bryan and the people. Dwayne usually talks to her near the end of the call. He tells her he loves her as he says goodbye.

I also try to call my son, Steven. I leave messages asking him to talk to me and to come visit me. He never calls me back. Tom has kept his promise to turn at least one of my children against me.

I can't wait for Stephanie to get here and away from him.

Finally, the day comes for me to drive to Austin to pick her up at the airport. Dwayne has delayed going on the road for his job, but he has to be at the REC building today. He's leaving soon on his first work trip to Baltimore for a hospital lab project.

Standing in the middle of the crowd at the airport gate, I search the faces of the people coming through the door. Finally, Stephanie shoves her way past a cluster of people. Her eyes are red from crying. I pull her stiff body against mine. "Are you okay?"

"No. I miss home already."

I step back. "You are home now."

She jerks away from me and turns her back on me as she moves down the escalator to baggage claim.

We walk without speaking to get her suitcase, and we begin our drive to Bryan. I chatter about how I've fixed up her room in the trailer. We've made one room for her bedroom and another for a separate room with a couch and a television. I add, "Your own little apartment."

"With no friends to visit." She turns away from me and fixes her eyes on the Texas fields and ranch gates out the window.

"You will make friends," I promise.

She shakes her head but doesn't say anything.

I continue, "You can go to Springfield to visit your old friends when you want."

"I hope they remember me."

Thirty minutes later, she breaks the tense silence. "I went to visit Dad."

I grip the steering wheel. "Did you? Do you want to tell me what happened?"

She turns away from the window and leans her head against the back of her seat. "I thought maybe I'd live with him until I graduated this year."

I swallow hard against the words rising in me. "I didn't know you were thinking about that."

"Yeah, I actually believed he could be a real dad."

I don't say anything, just reach over and take her hand. I grasp it in mine as I listen to her.

"He said he'd be glad to have me live with him." She rubs tears from her eyes and continues in a wavering voice. "Then he spent the night sitting by my bed crying and begging me to make you come home."

"Oh, Stephanie, I'm sorry."

"He said you're going to hell for divorcing him and marrying Dwayne."

I mutter a curse. "I promise you I never would've married Dwayne if I didn't think he'd be a good father for you."

"I know, Mom. But he's still a stranger to me." We drive the rest of the way in quiet agreement to stop talking about her father or Dwayne.

When we get to Bryan, we sit in the driveway. I observe her view the shabby trailer for the first time. She doesn't say anything; she just steps out of the car with an audible sigh.

Dwayne comes out of the garage to meet us. "Welcome home, Steph!"

She moves away from him when he tries to hug her. He grabs her suitcase from the car, following us into the house.

I point down the hall to the right, and she trudges down it

with Dwayne and me behind her. He drops her suitcase on the floor by the bed. He glances at me, and I nod my head to tell him it's okay. He walks out of the room and leaves the two of us standing in the middle of the small room.

She turns in a circle and takes in her posters and other items I've unpacked and put up. I've hung her curtains and put the same comforter from her Missouri bedroom on her bed in her new room. She walks into the next room, where we've wedged in a loveseat and a large bookshelf. Her stereo and a television sit on it, and she can fill the shelves with her CDs and books.

Finally, she smiles at me. "Thanks, Mom."

"Are you hungry? I made your favorite dinner. My fried chicken."

She thanks me but tells me she's not hungry and wants to call her friends now. I join Dwayne in the living room. We hear the door to her room shut and the murmur of her voice on the phone.

Two weeks later Dwayne leaves on his work trip. As I hug him goodbye, he hands me an envelope full of cash and tells me to put it in the bank. "Buy my girls clothes and stuff for school." He grins at me. "You'll probably buy a stack of books."

We talk every night on the phone. Stephanie and I explore our new hometown. With Jessica we shop the back-to-school sales. We sometimes drive aimlessly through the town and surrounding countryside, trying to make it feel less foreign.

Finally, Dwayne comes home. I spend most of my time sitting in a lawn chair in the garage, watching him work on his latest project: an electrical motorcycle. He's drawn his design on poster paper and hung it over the workbench. I help him pull parts off an old Honda motorcycle to use in his creation.

The radio plays classic country in the corner. "If the radio in the garage is playing, then you know I'm coming back to work here soon," he said when I asked why it's never turned off.   In the stifling heat of the garage, sweat saturates his T-shirt, and his oil-stained hands deftly weld and shape the metal pieces into a motorcycle. Occasionally, he waves his hands in the air and describes for me how the rear tire will rotate and produce energy. I don't understand any of it, but I'm satisfied sitting there on the stained concrete floor, handing him tools.

One morning Dwayne takes Stephanie to the Department of Public Safety, so she can transfer her driver's license to Texas. I'm staying home to complete my applications for teaching positions. School will be starting soon, and I still don't have a job.

Less than an hour later, I hear the truck doors slam. Stephanie bangs through the front door. Without looking at me at the kitchen table, she marches down the hall. Her door slams behind her.

Dwayne steps through the open door and closes it. I pour him a cup of coffee, and we lean across the table to talk, keeping our voices low.

He smooths his mustache with one finger. "They wouldn't give Steph her license." He takes a sip of coffee. "Said she had her license suspended in Missouri for not paying a speeding ticket."

I remember that ticket and start to answer him.

"I paid it!" We hadn't heard Stephanie join us.

I look up at her. "I gave you a check for it. You did go to the courthouse to pay it?"

She grabs the back of a chair, her fingers gripping it. "Mom." She stops.

Dwayne lays his hand over hers. "Stephanie told me she paid the ticket. She wouldn't lie to us." He turns to me. "One of my friends at the DPS called the Missouri Highway Patrol. The suspension order came from a Trooper Dave Johnson. You know him?"

The highway patrolman who once told me to go home to my husband. "Yeah, I know him," I say. "He's a friend of Tom's."

Stephanie drops into a chair. "Dad did this."

We sit in silence, and I wonder if I should tell her that her dad wouldn't do this to her. I can't.

Dwayne pulls out his cigarettes and grabs his phone. "You girls sit tight. I'll take care of it."

Stephanie and I drink one cup of coffee after another, listening to Dwayne talking on the phone. Through the window we watch him as he paces the deck with his cigarette in one hand. We hear the murmur of his voice with each new call.

Finally, he comes through the front door. He puts the phone back on its base. "Get your purse, Steph. Your Texas license is waiting for you at the DPS."

We stand up. I ask him, "How did you do it?"

He pulls his truck keys out of his pocket. "You just gotta know who to call."

Stephanie goes to get her purse. I smile at him. "I love you."

"Love you too. Told you I'd take care of you and Steph."

He walks out the door, and I stop Stephanie when she follows him. I stroke her cheek. "Are you okay?"

She hugs me for the first time in months. "You're right. Dwayne's a good dad."

A HARLEY MECHANIC
AGAIN

"**I** see, Mrs. Black, that you graduated from a college outside Texas." The principal looks over his glasses at me. "Are you aware of the teaching standards here in Texas?"

I know I will not be able to convince him I do. I try anyway. "I believe a good teacher can be one wherever she teaches." I point out that I was a recognized master teacher in Missouri and was teacher of the year in my district there. I add that I have now married a man who was born in Dallas and grew up here in Bryan.

He pushes his wire-rimmed glasses up onto his bristly gray hair, cut into a stiff crew cut. He leans forward and rests his elbows, in his crisp blue denim shirt, on the wooden table. With a glance at the rest of the interview committee around the table, he begins to flip through my application as he quietly reads it. The teachers and parents sitting around the table facing me also look down at the papers in front of them. A few take notes, and no one makes eye contact with me.

I shift on the hard wooden chair. I tug down my skirt under the table and feel the suit jacket bind across my shoulders. I take a deep breath, knowing I won't get the teaching job. This is my fifth interview for different school districts in Texas after my move here after our wedding three months ago. They always end with me explaining how an out-of-state teacher can be as good as a Texan.

Finally, the principal clears his throat with a rasp. "Thank you for coming in today. I'll call you in the next few days to let you know our decision." He pushes his chair back with a screech and moves around the table.

I stand and meet him at the door. He shakes my hand and opens the door. I walk out and hear one of the teachers on the panel speak as the door closes. "Too bad she isn't from here."

As soon as I get home, I kick off my heels and fling them into the back of the closet. I strip off the restricting suit and leave it on the bedroom floor. In my underwear, I stretch out on the bed and call Dwayne. He's working in a laboratory on Long Island.

I hear the humming of the fans in the lab in the background when he answers the phone. He asks me to wait while he steps outside. I hear the click of his lighter in a few minutes. I know he's smoking and talking on the phone, as always.

"How'd it go, baby?" His voice finally asks over the phone.

I close my eyes in frustration. "I'm sure I won't get the job. I still wasn't born a Texan."

He reminds me how good I am as a teacher. I hear him blow out smoke. "I wish I was there to tell you that in person. I miss you, Mary Jane Black." Hearing my new name always calms me.

I relax against the pillows. "I wish you were here too." I grip the phone in my hand. "I don't know what I'll do if I'm not teaching. Maybe you wouldn't have to be on the road so much if I had a paycheck."

"I gotta work, baby. You know I have to bring in money." We both remember the last time he lost a job and broke up with me as a result.

"Yeah, I know. I just miss you when you're gone."

"I'll be home tomorrow night."

I pick him up at the airport the next day, and he drives us home. I sit close beside him with his hand on my thigh, my skin under my cotton skirt warmed by his fingers.

He tells me about his work at the hospital in New York. With his words I can picture the cramped research laboratory. The clang of the cubicle doors. The doctors in their rumpled white coats. The smell of the bleach drying on the floor. He laughs when he describes how he recommended wine and Johnny Mathis music to a worried doctor for the rats who wouldn't mate.

I miss working with him on the road but know I need to be here with Stephanie, helping her adjust to the move in her senior year of high school.

Now I rest my head on his shoulder and laugh at his stories. The stress of job hunting and the strain of life in a strange new hometown melt away.

Soon we're pulling into the driveway of our new house. The house, sheltered by the spreading limbs of a gigantic live oak tree, has become a home for us and our daughters after I got money from selling the house Tom and I owned together. Dwayne and I traveled back to Springfield to sign the papers. The nervous realtor told us Tom refused to be in the same room as us. She walked back and forth between the rooms with papers for us to sign. Before she escorted Tom out the back door, she lowered her voice and told us how angry he had been to learn that Dwayne had to sign the papers as my husband. Now the money has given us a home for our newly created family.

Stephanie is sitting at the kitchen table when we come in the back door. She jumps up and hugs Dwayne. He tells her he's glad to be home with his girls. They sit down at the table, and she shows him her homework for her physics class. They chat about force and motion.

I cook dinner, listening to their conversation with a smile. He didn't finish high school and got his GED in his twenties. However, he knows how any machine works. Now he draws a hydraulic system for a piece of zoo equipment for Stephanie. She talks about the formulas and facts from math and science that go with each movement of the machine.

I carry the bowls and plates of food to the table. We eat and laugh in the brightly lit room with the dark Texas night outside the window.

The next morning I sit on a rolling mechanic's stool in the carport while Dwayne sits cross-legged on the oil-smeared concrete floor by a Cushman motor scooter he's rebuilding for a friend. I push myself forward into the sunshine, so I can read the small newspaper print of the classified ads. I read through the Help Wanted column while behind me Dwayne ratchets off the lug nuts of the Cushman wheels.

Suddenly a motorcycle swerves into our driveway with a scatter of gravel. The rider's long gray beard ruffles in the wind. I know by the beard that he is Dwayne's friend Pete, whom he's known since kindergarten. I ease myself off the stool. Dwayne stands by me, with a shop towel in his hand.

Pete snaps out his kickstand. As he steps off the bike, we see the woman behind him for the first time. She swings her right leg over the seat and jumps off the motorcycle. Her dark hair hangs in a long braid down her back. She pushes up her sunglasses, and we can see her bright blue eyes contrasted against her dark skin.

Pete introduces her as Doris and tells us he met her at the paint shop where he works. After hand shaking and introductions, Dwayne and Pete examine his new motorcycle: a Kawasaki. Doris and I smile at each other as they talk about engines and torque.

We chat while the men examine the motorcycle motor. She's

getting a degree in social work, and I talk about my teaching and my frustration about not finding a job here.

When the three of them form a smoking circle, I lean against our car and listen. Pete tells us he found out while motorcycle shopping that a Harley dealership has opened in Bryan. He adds that an old friend of Dwayne's bought it, Bruce Webber.

Dwayne says, "Bruce and me rode together when we were a lot younger. We took a lot of road trips. Sturgis and Daytona." He throws his cigarette on the ground and grinds it into the gravel. "Hell, I built Bruce's first Harley."

Dwayne laughs as he talks about how they stripped off the factory parts and threw them out. Now those parts are worth thousands of dollars.

They talk about all of the guys who rode Harleys with them years ago, about the time they met Paul Newman in a gas station on the way to Daytona Bike Week. The stories fly between them, each of them adding details and memories.

I listen to their shared motorcycle tales and realize again how much he has missed riding Harleys for the last fourteen years.

Eventually, Pete gets back on the motorcycle. Doris steps up on the passenger peg and maneuvers herself behind him. Dwayne and I watch them roll down the driveway and swing left onto the street with a roar. We both stand in silence and watch them disappear.

As the sun sets behind the tree in our front yard at the end of the day, we sit in our porch swing. Dwayne's arm drapes over my shoulders, and we rhythmically rock back and forth.

Dwayne takes a sip of iced tea with a click of ice. "What would you think of my going to the new Harley shop tomorrow and talking to Bruce about a job? That would take care of my being on the road so much."

I lean over and kiss him. "You'll be home every night," I say.

"I think I found a job in the classifieds. At the television station KBTX. Maybe those journalism classes in college will help."

He swivels around to face me. He holds his glass up for a toast. I clink mine against his. Together we chant, "To new jobs for both of us!"

I borrow Stephanie's car the next morning to go to the TV station to apply for the job. Dwayne drives our truck to the Harley shop to talk to Bruce. I push open the glass door with KBTX on it in gold-painted letters.

A tall woman behind the front counter with her stiff blond hair piled high on her head greets me with a smile. "Hello there! How can I help you?" she asks in her soft drawl as she faces me over the front counter.

I introduce myself and tell her I'm here about the job as a sales associate. She asks me to take a seat. She pushes some buttons on her telephone and tells someone I'm in the lobby. I wait for a short time. Then a tall thin man in a blue pinstriped suit walks briskly through the door. He sticks out his hand and I shake it. He tells me his name is John Bosworth. I tell him mine.

I follow him down a long hallway to his office. Pictures of John with what must be famous Texans, even though I don't recognize any of them but Ann Richards, crowd the walls, along with awards for outstanding news reporting. Haphazard piles of papers cover the surface of his desk. A cup of cold coffee sits on top of a book.

John drops down in his chair and swivels to face me. He jerks down the knot of his Aggie-maroon tie with the Texas A&M logo on it in an effort to loosen it. He takes off his jacket and rolls up his sleeves. He folds the jacket and searches for a place to put it. Then he drapes it over the phone. He pushes his hand through his thick blond hair, moving it away from his face.

He opens a drawer and begins to pull out sheets of paper,

adding them to the stack on his desk. Finally, he finds an application and hands it to me. I start looking for a pen in my purse.

"Hey, why don't we just chat, and then you can fill out the papers later?" He slaps his hand down on the nearest stack of paper on his desk.

I agree. He asks me some questions about my college courses and experience with newspapers or television. I tell him about my working for my college newspaper and my teaching high school journalism classes. He takes notes on a yellow legal pad. We laugh together at my story of the television newsman, my college professor and mentor, who terrified us with his bloody stories of covering wars around the world.

Finally, John leans back in his brown leather chair. "You are totally not suited for a sales associate job."

I nod in agreement and pick my purse off the floor. I start to stand up.

"Hey, I didn't say you had to leave."

I sit back down and look at him in surprise. I hold my purse against my chest and push my hair behind my ears in nervousness.

He offers me a job in the newsroom. He warns me it sounds way more glamorous than it is. I will be the assignment editor and assistant director of the morning news. He grins and tells me to think about it.

"You'll really be babysitting the morning anchor and answering the phone in hopes of a news story in a little Texas town. The biggest story last month was a possible bomb threat at the Walmart. Even that was a hoax."

I tell him I don't need to think about it. I accept the job on the spot. He walks me around the station and introduces me to people.

I rush home to tell Dwayne the news. His truck is sitting in the driveway when I get there. I run through the back door and shout the news that I got a job.

Dwayne joins me in the kitchen. "I'm the new Harley mechanic and parts guy at the Harley shop." We slap our palms in a high five. Harleys will now be a part of his life again. And mine.

Over dinner that night, Stephanie congratulates us on the jobs. She looks up from her plate and says, "I've met a really nice guy named John. I want you guys to meet him soon."

Dwayne says, "He's welcome here anytime."

The next morning Dwayne drives to the Harley shop. "You should come with me," he says. "You're going to be spending a lot of time around Harleys now."

We walk through the line of Harleys parked outside the building. A neon-orange Harley bar and shield gleams by the front door. I step through it and stare at the mass of motorcycles sitting side by side on the showroom floor. The fluorescent light bounces off the glossy gas tanks.

Dwayne takes my hand and points to a long counter at the back of the room. "That's the parts counter, baby. I'll be working there." He kisses my forehead. "Thanks for letting me be a Harley guy again."

I put my hand on his shoulder. "Remember, we agreed. Neither one of us lets the other do anything. We are partners, right?"

I was Tom's wife but never his partner. I asked his permission for my every move. Going to the store. Buying clothes. Eating dinner with friends. I woke up each morning wondering what mood he would be in.

Dwayne knows I'm thinking about my life with Tom and says, "I love you and want you to do whatever the hell you want to do."

Here on the Harley sales floor I take Dwayne's hand and squeeze it. He presses mine back.

A muscled, bearded man with thick curly red hair interrupts us. He sticks out his hand, and I shake it. He introduces himself as Bruce, the owner of the shop. He tells me, "Hiring Dwayne is the smartest thing I've done since I opened the door. He's kinda the godfather of Harleys here in Bryan. None of us could believe he stopped riding for over fifteen years."

After we chat with Bruce for a minute, Dwayne tells him he's going to take me into the shop to introduce me to the mechanics. We walk into the large, noisy space. Smoke hangs in the air from the exhaust pipes.

The rhythmic beat of rock music pours out of speakers hung on the wall. Motorcycles perch on lifts. The men working on them twist wrenches or drill off bolts with a burst of sound. Over the sound of the music and the tools, the mechanics laugh and shout at each other. We visited Harley mechanics during our days of working together before we were married. Now Dwayne will be working with them every day.

Raising his voice to be heard over the noise, Dwayne says, "I've known some of these guys since high school. I rode with most of the young guys' fathers."

One of the mechanics spots us and walks over to us. "Hey, I'm Wild Bill. I sure am glad to meet you. Dwayne told us all about you yesterday." He sticks out one hand, and tattoos curl around his muscled arm.

I shake his hand, and Bill yells at the other mechanics to come meet me. "Y'all come over and meet Dwayne's Mary."

SHOVELHEAD

On a July Sunday morning, Dwayne shoves his Thrifty Nickel paper toward me. "Look, baby, a 1980 FLT for only one thousand dollars!" We are sitting at the kitchen table and drinking our morning coffee. I am writing my community events calendar for the morning news at the Bryan television station, where I now work.

I peer at the tiny, blurry black-and-white picture of a motorcycle. "Is that a good deal?"

"It's a shovelhead!"

I am not aware of the unique features of shovelhead Harleys. He grabs one of my pencils, and in the margin of the paper, he draws a shovelhead engine as he describes its unique components. The defining feature is the top of the motor shaped like an overturned shovel blade. The shovel-shaped head brings more air into the motor. More oxygen increases the power of the motorcycle.

"After we get through with it, it will be fast as hell," he assures me. I will be his Harley mechanic apprentice. My experiences with him as his work assistant have helped us develop a rhythm of working side by side. I only hope I can learn about Harley motors.

Dwayne quickly calls the number in the paper. He worries

that such a good deal will evaporate if we don't jump on it quickly. We climb into his old Chevy pickup and drive out into the country where the man lives.

Hounds bark and jump wildly about our truck when we pull into the driveway of an old farmhouse badly in need of paint. An older man with a ring of white hair on his bald head comes out onto the porch. Dwayne and the man shake hands and exchange the usual Bryan greeting, which consists of establishing who your family is and where it fits into the social structure of the town. Bill is a fourth cousin of the guy Dwayne worked for ten years ago.

We walk through the high grass of the yard toward a large garage in the back. The garage is freshly painted bright blue, and as he swings open the door, I notice the spotlessly clean concrete floor and tools hung in neat rows around the room. Dwayne and Bill go to the corner of the room, and Bill pulls the canvas tarp off a large lump in the corner. It is the Harley. It is mostly red, and rust flakes off the chrome parts. Since this is an FLT, the motorcycle is a Harley bagger, which means it has metal saddlebags attached to the rear fender and a plastic curved front section called a fairing with a large windshield now cracked and yellow.

Dwayne squats down by the motorcycle and lays a reverent hand on the inverted pyramid of the motor. He looks at me, and I smile. We are going to buy the Harley.

Bill points to the Harley. "I bought that Harley when it was brand new. It was my first one."

"I've had over twenty Harleys. I haven't ridden since 1982, when my daughter was born—fifteen years now." Dwayne reaches out and draws me into their conversation by taking my hand and gently pulling me toward him. "My wife, Mary, and I are going to buy and build this one together. We made a promise on our wedding day to buy one."

"My wife is making me sell it," Bill says.

Dwayne and Bill shake hands on the selling price. Bill digs through a cardboard box at his kitchen table and finds the title. He signs it and hands it to Dwayne, who signs as the buyer of a 1980 Harley-Davidson FLHT. Dwayne insists I sign below his name, since we own this motorcycle together.

We load the Harley into the back of our truck and take it home. Dwayne puts the ramp against the tailgate, and I straddle the seat and roll it down the ramp. He guides it as it glides into the garage. It is my first time on a Harley since I rode on the back of one with a high school boyfriend.

For the rest of the day, we peel off parts of the motorcycle that will need to be painted or to be replaced. Dwayne rips off the useless windshield and throws it in the corner. He tells me that the guy who sold him his first Harley had to tear off the windshield for him. "I couldn't see over it, since I was thirteen and too short."

As I fix dinner that evening, he sits at the table with his drawing pad and sketches out the design for the finished motorcycle. He skillfully lines up the shape of the new gas tank and with a ruler aligns each angle of the frame to fit his new vision. He draws and tells stories of his Harleys over the years: the 1953 Panhead he rode during a freezing December from Washington State to Buffalo, New York; the first Shovelhead he owned; and the FLHT his second wife made him sell—one just like our new bagger.

Over the next weeks, we transform the shovelhead from a dusty wreck to the custom chopper Dwayne always saw beneath the outer shell. I learn how to remove a Harley motor and then to take apart each piece of it. Dwayne patiently explains how each part works together to be a unique Harley V-twin engine. He tells me the V shape allows the large, powerful engine to fit in a small space.

My hands soon match his. My fingernails are cracked, and

grease packs into every crevice of my hands and arms. I go to sleep at night with phrases like *spark plug gap*, *derby covers*, and *cylinders* running through my head.

His Harley mechanic buddies begin to hang out in our garage on Sundays to watch the transformation. Leaning against the wall with coffee cups in their hands, they offer occasional suggestions and praise. Most of the time Dwayne and I are alone together working side by side.

As the true Harley expert, he does the major mechanical work. He talks through each step of the process. He wants me to understand what he is doing. He says this will come in handy when I have my own Harley to build. His strong, muscled hands, scarred by years of slipped wrenches and screwdrivers, assemble the random pieces into a rebuilt motor.

I specialize in rewiring the headlights and turn signals. Using the Harley manual, I memorize the electrical circuit charts. It proves to be more difficult than deconstructing a Shakespeare play for students. Sometimes I sit in my lawn chair nearby and polish an endless pile of pitted chrome pieces.

Finally, four months later, we gaze in pride at our Harley-Davidson shovelhead motorcycle. Its ebony paint and the silver steel of the engine gleam in the fluorescent lights. Dwayne rolls the Harley into the driveway and prepares to fire it up.

"Baby, this is the moment we've been working for. When we know if the engine we built will fire up."

I give him a thumbs-up. "Turn the key!"

He turns the barrel key in the ignition on the gas tank and then pushes the starter button on the right handlebar. It starts. The motor rumbles in the morning air, and the signature *potato, potato* sound fills the air.

Dwayne places his hand on the throbbing gas tank. "Damn, she sounds good."

After the engine warms, Dwayne throws his leg over the seat and rolls the throttle forward. The motor roars. He takes it off the kickstand and skids forward slightly. I step up on the passenger peg on the rear wheel and slither my right leg behind him. I settle onto my part of the seat. He pushes backward until his spine is pressed against me. I wrap my arms around his slim waist. He lifts his feet and shifts it into first gear. We take off in a shower of gravel.

I feel the vibration of a Harley motor through my feet and thighs for the first time since I was seventeen. I bounce slightly with the bump of the tires on the gravel. As we pull onto the paved road, he increases the acceleration and gradually shifts up to fourth gear. At sixty-five miles per hour, I release my hold on Dwayne and swing my arms straight out. I close my eyes. I fly through the rushing air around me. Dwayne reaches back and lays his forearm on my leg. The fingers of his left hand curl over my knee. We speed down the highway joined together.

FATHERS
AND DAUGHTERS

The stinging drops of water bounce off the metal surface of the motorcycle and the asphalt pavement. The wetness creeps up my jeans under my leather chaps. Dwayne and I sit in the middle of his friends and coworkers with the rain pouring down on us and our Harley. The Santa hat I wore for the Christmas parade now hangs dripping down my shoulder.

Bruce thought it was a great idea to have all of his employees and their friends on motorcycles riding down College Avenue as part of the parade. The persistent thunderstorm has now ruined the holiday feeling for all of us.

I lean forward and whisper in Dwayne's ear, "How much farther is it to the end?"

"Too damn far. A hot motor and wet underwear are not a good combination." He rolls the throttle slightly. The motor complains with a damp *putt putt* sound. Around us the other motorcycles stutter and mutter in the heavy fall of water.

Suddenly our friend Pete rolls up beside us. "This old man is wet and tired. I need a damn beer." Doris, on the back of his motorcycle, and I look at each other. Her red-and-green bandana has slid down over the top of eyes. She peers out at the rain with mascara lines running down her cheeks. I laugh at the sight of her and know I look just as hopeless. She giggles and then laughs out loud. Water drips off the end of my nose.

Dwayne and Pete say in unison, "Let's get the hell out of here."

With a roar and a splash, we curve out of the line of motorcycles. The hot wind from the exhaust pipes shoots water onto the wheels. My legs become even more soaked with water. Behind me I hear Pete's motorcycle. Then one by one each of our friends joins us. We roll into the parking lot of a nearby bar. With military precision we back into spaces one after the other.

As our shovelhead tilts into the kickstand, Dwayne stands up to let me slide from behind him. My leather chaps pull away from the wet seat with a squish. I set my left foot on the pavement and into a water puddle. I hop sideways until my right leg edges off the back of the Harley.

Dwayne slings his arm around my shoulders and pulls himself off the bike. "How do you like the Harley life now, baby?" Water drips off his mustache. We grin at each other, and raindrops blast us.

Thirty wet bikers march into the bar. The hostess yells at a bus boy to bring a mop. We stand in the entryway and strip off our leather chaps, boots, and vests. A waitress brings us chairs, and leather soon drapes over them in a ghostly, black, dripping parade. The bus boy vigorously mops up the flood.

Pete yells, "Beers for everyone. We'll be back in a minute."

We slosh our way into the restrooms. I peel off my T-shirt, jeans, and socks. In my underwear I hold each one under the hot air hand dryer. I take my three minutes of drying time and begin drying myself off with the rolls of paper towels someone brought in their saddlebags. We all agree she is a genius.

Back in my warm, damp clothes, I walk back to the table

where Dwayne and Pete are sitting. Doris walks behind me as we weave among the crowded tables. We sit and watch the rain glide down the window while we drink and talk.

I look at the clock over the bar and see that it is almost six o'clock. I need to call Stephanie to let her know we're waiting for the rain to end or to at least let up before heading home. She invited her boyfriend, John, to the house while we rode in the parade. They were going to watch the parade on TV and then eat dinner with us.

Dwayne and I are glad that she has made some friends and found John. The move to Bryan the summer before her senior year meant she had to find new friends—never easy for any teenager. Now she has graduated from high school and has a job at a loan company owned by one of Dwayne's friends.

She seems happier, but we find it difficult to like John. He has helped Stephanie fit into her new town. I worry that she seems too anxious to please him. I know how that feels after being married to her father. Dwayne says he comes from *a first family of Bryan*, country club Catholics who own a big business in town.

I press the pay phone receiver to my ear and listen to the ringing on the other end. I wonder where my daughter is. I hope she and John didn't try to drive in the storm. A moment of mother worry washes over me. I walk back to the table and plop down in my chair by Dwayne.

He lays his hand over mine on the table. "How's Steph?"

"She didn't answer. I don't know where she is."

Over the next hour, I call her several more times. Still no answer.

I shake my head in frustration after returning to the table after the sixth call.

Dwayne stands up and pushes back his chair. "Let's go home."

We grab our leathers and begin to dress in the soggy chaps

and jackets. My boots stick to my socks when I try to push them on. Pete and Doris join us. We mount the wet motorcycles, and the water soaks into our almost dry clothes.

We ride into the wall of rain. I shield Dwayne's eyes with one hand in an attempt to keep water from dripping into his eyes. His goggles keep fogging up, and I use my finger to wipe them. Pete's motor mumbles beside us, but we are wrapped in a swirling gray mist and can't see him. We can only see our headlight glowing a few feet into the thick haze.

It is only five miles to our house, but it takes us almost an hour to get there. We stop to rest under trees and once under the awning of a closed gas station. As we turn onto the road to our house, Pete beeps goodbye and disappears into the murk and the water.

We pull into the carport, and our wet tires leave a path on the concrete. The rain bangs on the tin roof above us. We run to the back door and fall through it. Darkness fills the house. Stephanie isn't home.

As Dwayne makes coffee, I call the number for John's mother's house, where he lives. Stephanie was reluctant to give it to me, but I insisted. There is no answer there either. I hang up the phone and rest my hand on it. I wonder where she is in the rain and wind howling outside the house.

Over the next three hours, I call John's house over and over. No one ever answers. Dwayne offers to go look for her in the truck, but I remind him we have no idea where to look.

We finally lie side by side on the couch. The TV flickers in the dark room.

Dwayne's breath ruffles my hair. "John ain't going to get away with this shit. He should know how much we'd worry about our daughter."

We drift off to a restless sleep.

The bang of the back door wakes us. I sit up and look at the mantle clock. Two in the morning. Dwayne jumps off the couch and marches to the kitchen. I follow behind him. He flips on the light switch, and Stephanie stares at us in surprise at the burst of light.

I grab her and hug her tightly. "Do you have any idea how worried we were? Where the hell have you been?"

She pushes me back and tells me she was with John. They watched a movie at his house and fell asleep. "I'm going to bed. We can talk about this in the morning." Her bedroom door slams behind her.

Dwayne and I glance at each other.

I apologize for my daughter's behavior. "I guess being the parent of a teenage daughter is never easy. When you married me, you got another one in the deal."

He reaches out and grabs me. "She's my daughter too, you know."

We stagger with exhaustion to bed. The alarm wakes us three hours later, since we both have to go to work.

I take a cup of coffee to Stephanie's room and turn on the light. She moans as she wakes up to the glare. She mutters, "Fuck, Mom."

I hand her the coffee and tell her to meet us at the kitchen table in five minutes. She stumbles into the kitchen and falls into a chair. She holds the cup of warm coffee against her chin to let the steam warm her face.

"You know we love you, but you can't treat us the way you did yesterday." Dwayne reaches out and takes her hand. "We worry about you and need to know you're okay."

I take her other hand. "I always worry when I don't know where you are."

She blinks against her sudden tears. I reach up and smooth back her hair. She pulls down the sleeve of her shirt and wipes her nose. I smile at the childhood gesture.

"I love you guys too. I'm sorry." She takes a deep breath. "John and I decided last night we're going to get married. In February."

Dwayne starts to say something. I stop him with a touch of my hand on his. I gaze into Stephanie's eyes. "I married your father at eighteen, and it was a terrible mistake. You and your brother are the only good things I got out of it. Please wait until you're a little older."

She sets down her mug with a thud. "I am not you. John is not my father. You can't stop me." She glares at me defiantly.

Tears blur my vision. "You're probably right. I never listened to my mom."

The three of us sit in silence as the voices on the TV news murmur in the background. She goes back to bed and leaves us both sitting at the table. I get up and sit across Dwayne's legs. I wrap my arms around him and lay my head on his shoulder. He rocks me gently as the sun rises in a blaze of pink and gold. The clouds fade away from yesterday's storm.

Christmas rushes by in a rush of family dinners and holiday parties. We ride in the Toy Run hosted by Dwayne's Harley shop and give gifts to children when the pack of bikers stop at houses. At the end of the Toy Run, we meet Stephanie at the country club for a dinner with John and his parents, Susan and John Senior. John Senior tells us to call him Johnny. They are divorced but announce they are still friends and parents to their boys. I can't imagine saying that about Stephanie's father.

Dwayne and I sit in our Harley T-shirts and jeans across a starched white tablecloth from Susan and Johnny in their elegant suit and dress. John and Stephanie try to keep the conversation going. We eat a little of the expensive and tasteless food and go home to eat a bacon-and-fried-egg sandwich.

On New Year's Day, Stephanie calls her dad to tell him the news. Dwayne and I watch her through the door of the living room when she talks on the phone. We can hear his shouts through the receiver. We also hear *Dwayne* repeated multiple times.

Finally, Stephanie raises her voice in anger. "You're my father, so I want you to be at my wedding. Dwayne will be giving me away." She slams down the phone and drops down by me on the couch.

Dwayne asks her if she's sure.

"Yeah, I am." She leans back. "Would you want to walk me down the aisle?"

He jumps up and pulls her to her feet. He hugs her. "I'd be damn proud to do it."

The ring of the phone interrupts the moment. Stephanie's hand trembles as she holds the clanging phone. She looks at the answer button, afraid to push it.

Dwayne takes it from her hand and answers it. "We haven't talked since that day at your house, but it's about time we did it again." He walks out of the room with the receiver against his ear. We hear the front door slap shut. Then the porch swing squeaks as he sits down.

I squeeze her hand. "I'm happy but a little surprised you want Dwayne to walk you down the aisle."

She lays her head on my shoulder. "You know I was mad when you moved me here, but I started to notice all Dwayne talked about was what he could do for me. How he could make me happy. All Dad ever did was worry about himself. And me keeping him happy."

We sit and strain to listen to the murmured voice on the porch. Eventually, we hear Dwayne say he'll call him back after we all talk.

He walks into the living room and clunks the phone down on its base. He sits in his recliner and leans over his knees. "He will be at the wedding, and he will pay for it as your father." He stops and looks at Stephanie. "He'll only pay for it if he walks you down the aisle."

All of us sit frozen as we consider the ultimatum. Dwayne

and I know that we can't afford the wedding John's parents will expect. I also know that Dwayne will sell and barter whatever he can to try to make it happen. But it will not be possible for us to find that kind of money.

Stephanie sits down by me on the couch. "I don't know what to do. I haven't seen him in three years. Why does he even want to walk me down the aisle?"

"It is all about the winning." Dwayne sits up straight in his chair. "I never backed down from a fight, but I'll do whatever you want."

Stephanie tells us she has to think about what to do. We agree she needs time.

Two days later at breakfast she tells us she has made her decision. She asks Dwayne to talk to her about it. They go outside and sway back and forth in the porch swing. I hear the rise and fall of their voices.

I look up from the morning newspaper when they return to the kitchen.

Dwayne lays his hand on my shoulder. "She knows we aren't able to pay for the wedding, but she refuses to let him walk her down the aisle. She's going to walk down the aisle by herself."

I stand up and pull both of them to me. We hug each other for a long moment until it is time to go to work and to school. We know her father will not accept her decision without a fight.

When we get home that night, we sit down to dinner. We don't speak as we sit around the table. Dwayne lays down his fork with a clank. We look up at him in surprise. He pulls a bulky envelope from his back pocket. He hands it to Stephanie. She opens it to find a thick stack of money inside.

He tells us he has pawned some of his tools to put together some money for the wedding. He grins at us. "Go buy yourself a wedding dress."

THE DANCE

Two years have passed since I've seen my son Steven. On Stephanie's wedding day, I do. He slips into the hard wooden pew in front of me with his daughter, Danielle, and keeps his face turned away from me and my mother, who sits by my left side. Now he sits directly in front of me. His rigid back in his black suit communicates his simmering anger.

Danielle climbs up on the seat, and her small body leans across the back of it toward my mother. She does not know it is her great grandmother. Mom knows she is her great granddaughter. She reaches out and takes her tiny, delicate hand. Danielle laughs. She stretches out her arms.

Suddenly Steven swerves around to face us. He jerks Danielle away from Mom. He plops her down on his lap. He turns his back to us again. Danielle cries loudly. The small crowd in the Catholic church stares at us for a moment. I glance at Mom. Tears drip down her face. I hand her a tissue, and she smears her makeup as she wipes them off.

A voice whispers, "Mary, I hope you're happy." I look up to see Tom standing by me. His hand clutches the edge of the back of the bench, his knuckles white with the force of his grip.

I feel Dwayne on my right begin to rise, but I place my hand on his arm. He drops back down onto the seat.

It is the first time I have seen Tom since the day I brought my new husband to his house. I stare at Tom without speaking until he moves forward to sit with Steven. He lays one hand on our son's shoulder.

Music fills the chapel, and the moment of tension passes. We stand and turn to face the back of the church.

Two of Stephanie's friends stroll slowly down the aisle. Their pale pink dresses glow in the candlelight. Stephanie steps into the doorway.

The organ music rises in volume. Stephanie reaches down and pushes back the stiff white lace of her dress. She steps forward and paces down the aisle.

When she comes to reach the row where we are standing, Stephanie stops. We look at each other and smile. Dwayne sticks out his hand, and she clasps it for a moment.

In front of me, Tom turns and glares at me. I see his jaw muscles clenching beneath his skin. Dwayne and Stephanie let go of each other. She continues her march up to the altar. I hear the whispers as people steal quick glances at us, trying to figure out what just happened.

She reaches the altar and puts her hand on John's arm. The priest raises his hand. He asks who gives this woman in marriage. Dwayne, Tom, and I answer in unison that we do, but we avoid looking at each other. Tom keeps his back turned to us.

The wedding proceeds without incident. Near the end the priest asks Stephanie and John to sit on the front pew. I tense. This is not part of the traditional wedding mass.

The priest raises his hand as if he is blessing us. "I would like to talk about the sacred nature of marriage." Both the groom's and the bride's side of the church hold their breath. Each side contains a divorced mother and father. "This new marriage will bring the pieces of two broken families together. Their love will unite all of them as one family."

I stare at my son and my granddaughter and blink furiously to keep the tears back. Danielle's large blue eyes stare at me over Steven's shoulder. Tears still fill them from her crying. They are her father's eyes. They are my mother's eyes. Dwayne reaches over and takes my hand. He gently rubs his thumb across my palm.

At the front of the chapel the priest motions Stephanie and John to join him again at the altar. He firmly pronounces them man and wife. They walk quickly down the aisle.

Still holding hands, Dwayne and I start to follow them. Steven and Tom push past us and exit the church. We follow them with Mom bringing up the rear. We drive in silence to the country club for the reception.

The overpowering smell of roses fills the dining room at the club. Each parent of the newlyweds collects a small circle of family and friends around them. Our side contains several friends in black leather vests and motorcycle boots. Long beards are neatly trimmed today. They have slicked back their hair into tight ponytails. Women in silk dresses with glittering diamonds and men in custom-fitted tuxedos fill the groom's side.

Nervous laughter rings out now and then. The bartender keeps busy filling up glasses from the margarita machine. Stephanie and John circle among the tables.

Music soon fills the room from a small group of musicians who have set up at the front. "Ladies and gentlemen, it is time for the bride's dance with her father."

Tom and Stephanie stand in front of the band and then turn to face each other. The band plays a Sinatra song. Slowly, Tom and Stephanie dance around the floor in carefully measured steps. Stephanie's stiff hand lies on her father's shoulder.

Suddenly, the music changes. "Amarillo by Morning." George Strait. Stephanie steps away from her father. I realize Dwayne has moved to the front of the room. He and Stephanie join hands. They smile at each other. They gracefully begin to move rhythmically into the intricate steps of the Texas two-step. The white lace of her dress pools over his dark cowboy boots. Dwayne says something to her, and she laughs softly.

Tom backs away and turns on his heel. The door slams behind him as he leaves the room.

Steven begins to follow his father. I grab his elbow when he passes by me, and he swerves to face me. "You planned this, didn't you? It's not enough that you humiliated Dad by leaving him."

He adds that he will never forgive me for marrying again so soon.

He shakes off my hand on his arm. His face whitens, and I recognize the fierce face of his father that I saw often during our marriage.

"Steven, please," I beg him. I keep my voice low, so it can't be heard above the music.

He pushes me back against the table. A glass falls and spills its contents onto the starched white tablecloth. He rushes out of the room, and I follow him. Behind me George Strait sings about being home by morning. My daughter and husband share a dance.

In the hall Steven stops with a lurch. He turns to face me, and he clenches one hand against his leg. "How could you leave me?"

"I didn't leave you. I left your father." I start to reach out to wipe his tears away but drop my hand.

"Women," he spits out. "You're all alike." I stare at him in confusion.

He wraps his hand around my forearm and grips it tightly.

Pain shoots up my arm. "Didn't you wonder why Danielle's mother isn't with us? Oh, yeah, probably not. You have your new husband to worry about." He drops my arm. "Well, she left me too. Just walked out the door for a new man. Both of you. Whores."

He moves closer until his face is inches from mine. "Leave me the hell alone."

The outside door opens. Sunlight pours into the hall. We turn and see Tom in the doorway. He scowls at both of us, and I press myself against the wall. My heart beats loudly in my ears while an old fear fills my throat.

Tom strides down the hall and into the dining room. Steven follows him. My son turns to look at me before he enters the room. His lips move. I want to believe he says he's sorry.

I rub my arm where his fingers have left angry red marks. I go back to the dining room. Dwayne and Stephanie are sitting at the table with my mom and his mother, Roberta. Dwayne waves his hands through the air as he talks. The margarita in his glass sloshes up and down the sides. Everyone is laughing at his story.

Dwayne looks up and waves to me to come join them. I weave my way through the crowded tables. When I reach our table, Dwayne stands up and hugs me. He bends down and looks at my face closely, sensing something is wrong.

"Did you see our dance, Mom?" Stephanie asks. I smile and nod.

I lean and whisper in Dwayne's ear, "Please can we get out of here for a minute?"

Without speaking, he takes my hand and leads me out of the room. We sit in our car in the parking lot. I tell him about my confrontation with Steven. I calm his angry response. We just join hands for several minutes.

He reaches for a cigarette. I fix my makeup. We go back inside. After Stephanie and John leave for their honeymoon, we stand at the front door and watch people leave. Tom and Steven are among the first to go. They pass us without speaking. Steven straps Danielle into her car seat, and then they drive away. I doubt I will ever see my son again.

THE BRIDGE

The old man rubs his head, which is barely covered by his thin, fine white hair, and then he waves his gnarled brown hand toward a highway sign. "The suspension bridge is down that road. Over by San Saba." He removes the gas nozzle out of his truck and clangs it back into the pump. "I think so, anyway. Ain't never been there myself."

We have been chasing the first suspension bridge in Texas all morning. Dwayne and Pete saw a story about it on *Texas Country Reporter*. They decided it would be a fun day road trip for the four of us.

Dwayne and I are looking forward to a day together on the Harley after Stephanie's wedding three months ago. We have been busy helping the newlyweds get settled in their new house.

I have been trying to forget my confrontation with my son and my first husband at the wedding.

Our two motorcycles swerved out of our driveway at seven that morning, me on the back of our shovelhead and Doris behind Pete on their Kawasaki. In a carrier on the back of Pete's bike, their Chihuahua, Oscar, watches the passing scenery. Our Texas map matched with Dwayne's scrawled notes and hastily sketched map from the TV show serve as our only guide.

Now the midday sun blasts down on us. Doris and I sit on the curb at the gas station in the shade of the awning and watch Pete and Dwayne talking to the old man. Oscar drinks water out of a small plastic bowl and stretches out between us. The man waving out the directions is the fourth person we've asked about the bridge.

In Temple a skinny woman with a Marlboro dangling from her lips was sure the bridge was over by Lampasas. The two teenagers there kicked up their skateboards and told us they had studied about it in school. "Definitely in Brownwood," they declared with certainty.

In Brownwood a bent and frail old woman in a grocery store parking lot told us a story about the time she and her husband took their kids to the bridge. As Dwayne loaded her groceries in her car, she told us it was absolutely in San Angelo.

At the station in San Angelo, after getting more directions from the man at the gas pumps, I wiggle my toes inside my boots in an effort to ease the numbness. The pounding Harley engine under me has partially paralyzed my legs and feet. My butt aches from sitting on the narrow seat for five straight hours. I have never been happier.

I wrap my bandana around my windblown, knotted hair. Dwayne straddles the Harley and stands up to let me climb on behind him. I hop my leg over the seat, perching my prickling feet on the passenger pegs again. Beside me Doris performs the same balancing act. With a roar and a jolt, we swing left down the road the old man showed us. He waves at us as we pull out of the parking lot.

Either by luck or with good directions, we see a sign declaring the Beveridge Bridge on a road outside San Angelo. We follow the signs until we finally see the bridge arching over the San Saba River. The single-lane wood-and-iron pipe bridge stands out against the flat, arid landscape of West Texas.

We stop in the middle of the wooden planks on the bridge and look at the muddy brown river water chugging slowly over the rocky river bed. Doris jumps off and takes some pictures of us to commemorate our reaching our destination. We park on the narrow band of gravel on the other side of the bridge. We wipe sweat from our foreheads as we read the plaque on one of the arches on the bridge. *Built by the Flinn-Moyer Bridge Company, 1896.* As Dwayne and Pete smoke, they tell Texas history stories to Doris—a Louisiana girl—and me, a girl born in the Ozark Mountains.

Doris interrupts the stories to point out a small hand-painted wooden sign nailed to a fence post: *Bubba's Texas BBQ and cold beer.* A red arrow points up the road. *One half mile ahead.* We get back on our motorcycles and hope Bubba is still in business. We see the small wooden shack when we veer around a corner.

Soon we are relaxing on a picnic table with icy Shiner Bock beers and plates of ribs and brisket. Oscar growls at the owner's pit bull from his position under our feet.

I phone my principal, Joe, from the pay phone on the side of the BBQ joint to let him know I won't be chaperoning the prom tonight as planned. I got my first Texas teaching job when I met Joe on his Harley at a motorcycle rally. Dwayne introduced us. Now Joe tells me to have a beer for him, and he'll find another teacher to chaperone.

We sit there under the shade of the towering live oak trees the rest of the afternoon. At one point, Bubba joins us and shares a beer. Dwayne tells him the story of our search for the bridge. I watch him spin his tale with a wave of his arms.

Bubba spits out a long stream of tobacco juice and laughs.

"Hell, boy, the first suspension bridge in Texas is in Waco. That's probably the one on the TV. You four sure as shit were lost. A little ignorant too."

We all join in the laughter at our stupidity.

Dwayne drinks some beer and says, "Any day on two wheels is a good day."

Bubba agrees, "Hell yeah, I wish I still had my Harley."

We hoist ourselves back on the motorcycles. The two motorcycles rumble together down the two hundred miles home. We stop for gas at a station in a small town somewhere in the middle of the endless Texas plains. Doris and I stretch out in the dried grass beside the parking lot while the men fill the tanks, and Dwayne buys his lottery ticket with his lucky numbers. It's midnight when we pull into our driveway. Pete and Doris honk goodbye as they continue on to their own house.

Home at last, I pull my boots off my tired feet and set them by the door. I pull off my Harley overalls and sling them over a kitchen chair. Dwayne pours us each a glass of iced tea. We're walking through the living room on the way to the bedroom when I notice the blinking light on the answering machine.

I push the button as I sip my tea. A man's voice identifies himself as Dr. Gilmore. "I don't know if you remember me, but I performed your mother's last two cancer surgeries. I admitted her to the hospital today. Please call me as soon as possible."

I hear Dwayne turning on the water in the bathroom, and I stand there frozen in the dark. The warmth of the day has left me.

SECURITY

We're on our way home from my mother's funeral, an eight-hour drive. Night has fallen, and a blanket of darkness surrounds us, occasionally broken by flashes of light from passing cars. The sound of old-time country music plays softly on the radio with intermittent bursts of static.

I lean my head back against the headrest. A trip to see my mother in the hospital after the call from her surgeon has ended three weeks later in her death. I did not leave the side of her hospital bed for more than an hour or two through the pancreatic cancer diagnosis and surgery. Now my bones ache. My eyes burn.

Mom begged me to get Steven to visit her. I finally went to his work to ask him to see her after he never returned my calls. I even promised him I'd leave so he could talk to her alone. He told me he was done with both of us and walked away. I told Mom he wouldn't come. At her funeral, I held Dwayne's hand by her graveside with Stephanie by my side and hoped Steven had heard my call about the funeral and would have a change of heart. He never came.

I have never felt so exhausted or so alone in the world. My father killed himself twenty-three years ago, and now my mother has died from cancer. I am truly an orphan now.

Dwayne reaches out and grabs my hand, rubbing his thumb lightly across the back of it. "Do you remember the first time I met your mom? She must have cooked a whole cow for that stack of steaks." He releases my hand and lights a cigarette.

We listen to Hank Williams singing about being lonesome for a few minutes.

Dwayne powers down the window with a click. "I quit my job at the Harley shop," he tells me. "I know it seemed like the perfect job for me, but it just didn't work out."

He waves the hand with the cigarette through the space between us as he describes the custom motorcycle shop he wants to open in a few weeks. "I found the perfect building for it in College Station. It has a space in the front for bikes ready to sell and a huge work area where I can put the lifts and tools." He weaves his dreams through the dim light inside the car.

"Wait. Stop." I put my hand on his arm. He throws the cigarette out the window. "We just sold the house to avoid paying a balloon payment on the mortgage. How are we going to make it on just my teacher's salary?" This year I returned to teaching both because I missed it and because it was a steady source of income. Now it will be our only paycheck.

He assures me he will work on people's cars and motorcycles until his shop makes money. "I just can't work for Bruce anymore, baby. I can't put up with his shit. That should have been my Harley dealership." He reminds me that he still has his prototype for an electric motorcycle in the garage. "It'll make us both rich."

I turn in the seat and face the window, rubbing my itchy eyes. I feel as if I'm floating adrift in space.

The silence stretches between us. Dwayne lays his hand on my neck. "Talk to me, please."

A flood of fear and worry pours out of me. "We have no house. We are driving my daughter's cast-off car." Then I take a deep breath and whisper, "I couldn't even pay for Mom's funeral. I had to set up payments on it since we have less than a hundred dollars in the bank."

Anger and disappointment hang in the air. Dwayne moves his hand away from me and grips the steering wheel. "I thought you knew I'm not the kind of guy who retires from thirty years at the same job." He moves away from me. "I guess now you also know why you're my third wife."

We don't speak for the rest of the trip. The only sound is tires humming down the pavement. Hours later we arrive home, and we fall into bed. I sleep far on my side. He sleeps across the gap on the other side. It is the first time we haven't wanted our skin touching each other in the bed.

When the alarm buzzes the next morning, I forget in my anger not to wake him by touching him. His nightmares have ended, and he hasn't talked about Vietnam since that first drive to Bryan together. But any sudden physical contact in his sleep triggers an old war response. I have learned to wake him with my voice, not my touch. Now, in the early morning light, I reach out and shake Dwayne's arm to wake him.

He leaps from the bed and swings his arms wildly. Suddenly, he realizes he's home with me, not on a battlefield. "God damn it, Mary. I thought I was through with this shit." He stomps into the bathroom.

I sit on the bed and lean on my bent knees. My secure life seems shaky in the morning light.

The following days are spent packing. The first thing Dwayne wraps in newspaper and places in boxes is his collection of Harley memorabilia displayed in the wooden cabinet built by his great-uncle. Dwayne stripped off years of paint and varnish to stain it ebony with a hand-painted Harley bar and shield at the top. We have added some of the things we've bought at Harley shops across the country. The buckles from my first pair of Harley boots are the door handles.

We will need to move out of the house in a few weeks. Our first house together. The giant live oak tree shading the front porch. The barn turned into Dwayne's garage, where the radio is always on. A room I turned into my library with three walls of bookshelves Dwayne built. It has been sold, but we haven't found anywhere to live yet. My stomach knots at the thought of no house waiting for us. I don't know where we'll live.

One morning after a silent breakfast, Dwayne suggests I visit Stephanie. She and her new husband live a few miles away. Grateful for some time away from the packing and tension, I grab my keys. I pull out of the driveway and head to her house within minutes.

But I don't go to Stephanie's house. I drive out to the Brazos River and get out of the car. I stumble down the rocky riverbank to the edge of the water. I plop down on a flat sandy rock and stare at the murky water. I pick up a small rock from the ground and pitch it into the gurgling brown water. It sinks with a small plop. I picture my mom's face at the moment she stopped breathing.

The Texas sun beats down on my head, and I wonder how I can move past my fears about money. I continue to throw stones into the murky Brazos and think about hiding money for years to escape Tom. I remember lying awake in the night listening to his heavy breathing and wondering if I could find a safe place for Stephanie and me to live. I thought all I'd need was money and a house to be happy.

I think of that first night in Dwayne's trailer as his wife, safe and loved by him, and looking at the stack of money in his drawer. We promised then not to let money come between us. I remember his pawning his tools to buy Stephanie a wedding dress. I whisper most nights as we fall asleep, "You are my home."

I drive back to our house earlier than planned. I'm determined to talk through my worries about money with Dwayne. I need to tell him I know I'm lucky to have found him.

As my car pulls into the driveway, I notice him and another man standing there. Our shovelhead Harley gleams in the sunshine between them. Dwayne reaches out and hits the starter button. The motor roars. The man squats in the gravel and peers closely at the motor.

I park quickly. Pebbles flies from beneath my tires. Dwayne and the man turn to watch me walk toward them. "Hey, what's going on?"

Dwayne looks me in the eye. "I'm selling the shovelhead. Darrell here has always wanted it."

"The shovelhead is half mine, you know."

"Baby, we will get another motorcycle. We need the money."

Darrell shifts uncomfortably in the dirt. He stands up and steps back slightly. He avoids looking at either of us.

I lean against one of the carport metal pillars and watch them. Dwayne switches off the motorcycle. He runs his hand down the metallic black paint on the extended gas tank. He tells Darrell how we welded it together. He describes for him each step of our rebuilding process.

He finishes his description, "This scooter means a lot to me. It's our first one together." He glances quickly at me, then turns away.

None of us speak. We don't make eye contact. Dwayne gently rubs a smudge on the front fender. He looks at me again and tries to smile. I know he's trying to cheer me up.

Suddenly, Darrell reaches in his pocket and pulls out a large stack of money. Hundred-dollar bills. He begins to count them and lay them in Dwayne's palm. Dwayne looks at me. "He's giving me five thousand dollars for the shovelhead. We're going to be okay now."

I push myself off the metal column and join them. I tell Darrell the motorcycle isn't for sale after all.

He shakes his head and says it's the damnedest thing he's ever seen. Usually it's a woman who wants to sell the Harley. "Are you sure?" He turns to Dwayne.

Dwayne hands him the money back. "She's the boss." He grins. A real grin.

Darrell slams the door of his truck as he gets in it. He backs up with a stony flurry and drives quickly out of the driveway.

We face each other across the Harley. Dwayne wipes a tear from my face with one finger.

"I can't mess this up."

"You won't."

"Close your eyes."

I do as he says. I lay my hands on the motorcycle seat, and he covers them with his. I feel his rough battered hands against mine.

"Where do you see us living? Some place other than this town, where you have to live with my past."

I think about all of the places we've traveled and worked. One picture falls from the panorama. "Northern California. San Francisco. I've wanted to live in California since I spent my summers there as a teenager."

"Then that's where we'll go when we get our stuff into the storage place. I know a guy who works at a motorcycle parts place in Morgan Hill. That's closer to San Jose. Will that be okay?"

I agree that Morgan Hill sounds perfect. I remind him that teachers can always find a job.

"If we got each other, there's nothing we can't do." He moves around the motorcycle and hugs me tightly. "Thanks for saving the shovelhead. It was breaking my heart to sell her."

On the Sunday before we drive to California to find jobs and a place to live, we go to Roberta's house for one last Sunday dinner with his mom and his brother, Doug, before we leave. Doug and Dwayne hang out in the garage most of the day, sharing stories about all the times they traveled together for Dwayne's job. Roberta and I sit, watching an endless stream of cooking shows, since there are no game shows on the weekend. We talk about working in schools. She was the cook at an elementary school for over twenty years, and she's always fascinated by my work with high school–aged students.

On the way home, Dwayne rolls down the window to allow the smoke from his cigarette to drift out into the wind. With one hand, he reaches into his jeans pocket and pulls out an envelope. He tosses it into his lap. "Open it up, baby."

I lift the flap and pull out a check. Dwayne's name is on it, and it's for $10,000. His mother's signature is at the bottom. I turn to him and say, "What's this for?"

He flicks the cigarette out the window and says, "Mom wanted us to be able to get whatever we needed for our new life in California. She said you were the best thing that ever happened to me, and you shouldn't have to worry about money when we move."

On a warm afternoon four weeks later, we unload the Harley shovelhead out of the back of a U-Haul truck at our new house in Morgan Hill. He holds the ramp as I roll it slowly down the steep incline into the garage. I push out the kickstand with my toe. The motorcycle leans into its new home.

Dwayne plugs in his garage radio first, the way he does every time we move. He turns it on. "The music is on, so now this is my garage."

Jim Reeves floats into the space. We laugh as we recognize it as the song we danced to on our blind date.

"They're playing our dance song, baby." He pulls me into him. We dance and glide as we two-step across the dusty floor.

CALIFORNIA DREAMS

1999-2010

Love doesn't make the world go 'round.
Love is what makes the ride worthwhile.

FRANKLIN P. JONES

POLICE SPECIAL

I celebrate my forty-seventh birthday earning my motorcycle license. I straddle the small Honda Rebel and grip the handlebars. I lay my left hand on the clutch and pull in the brake with my right. I have practiced swerving and dipping around the plastic orange cones of the riding course for two weekends. The morning sun rising over the mountains behind me warms my shoulders through my leather coat. My head bobbles from the weight of the full helmet I'm required to wear. The rider before me finishes the course.

Last night I talked to Stephanie on the phone, and she told me she tells her friends, "If my mom can ride a Harley, she can do anything." I use that thought to boost my confidence now.

I pull in the clutch lever and shift up to first gear with my toe. I look at my instructor, who's writing on his clipboard. He studies me, astride the bike. I nod, and he raises his hand. I lift my left foot onto the peg, resting the weight of the bike on my right foot. He lowers his hand. I accelerate by rolling my right hand forward on the throttle. I take off with a jerk.

I soon get into the rhythm of riding. Accelerate. Lean right. Shift up. Lean left. Shift down. Pump brake. I stop with a tire squeak at the finish line. My instructor, Bill, smiles at me. He knows how nervous I am as the oldest member of the class. He writes my score onto the sheet on his clipboard and then he hands it to me. Ninety-five is written in red at the top. "Highest score in the class."

I'm ready to ride my first motorcycle solo. An hour later I run in the back door of our small duplex. "I passed with the highest score!"

Dwayne is sitting with a glass of iced tea in front of the television. He jumps up and hugs me. "Let's go roll that Honda out of the garage."

We walk down the sidewalk to the garage behind the duplex. With a push of the remote button, the door opens. A small black motorcycle squats beside his Harley. Dwayne bartered some mechanic work for the Honda Shadow. He said he knew I would get my license and needed a motorcycle. I have sat on it every evening, getting used to it. Under his guidance I customized it by switching out some of its Honda components and putting Harley parts on it. I made sure I put a new exhaust on it for the signature Harley sound. He calls it my Hardly Davidson.

He hands me a helmet and gloves he bought me at work. I swing my leg over the Honda and roll it backward down the slope of the driveway. Dwayne fires up his Harley, and we ride to a nearby commuter parking lot. I practice turns and shifting for an hour until it is too dark to continue.

Dwayne sits on a bench by the train platform and watches me. As the darkness settles over us, I see the tip of his cigarette glowing each time I pass.

For the next few months, I ride every afternoon after I finish teaching each day at the nearby high school, and we ride side by side on the straight and curved highways near our town on the weekends. I brave the San Jose traffic one Saturday afternoon and ride to meet Dwayne at the downtown Harley dealership where he works. I shut off the bike and roll it back into the line of Harleys by the front door. The big motorcycles dwarf it. I get off and walk into the store.

My helmet swings in my right hand and bumps against my knee. A line of gleaming motorcycles stretches in front of me. I perform my usual ritual of walking through them and picking the one I might want. I'm ready to move from the Honda to a Harley. Since I am well known in the shop, I can sit on a bright red motorcycle near the front door to see how it feels without finding a salesman. I push back the kickstand and lean it against my right leg. I realize the seat is too high for my short legs. I quickly put the kickstand back down.

I continue to walk down the line of Harleys. I stop in front of a Sportster, the smallest bike Harley makes. Most Harley riders call it a "'girl's bike" because of its small size and light dry weight. One of my friends from the motorcycle class has one. We spend a lot of time picking it up after it falls over on corners. It may not weigh as much as other Harleys, but it is top-heavy.

I feel Dwayne walk up behind me and wrap his arms around me. "You don't want a Sportster, do you?"

I agree that I don't. He asks me if I trust him to find me a Harley.

"Of course I do!"

"I will put you on a bike that will fit you like a glove. You don't need to limit yourself to a small Harley just because it's what other people say you should ride. You can ride any damned Harley you want." He's going to bring one he's found for me home next weekend, but he wants to keep what model it is a secret until I see it.

The next Saturday I'm sitting on the sidewalk in front of the garage. A red bandana is tied tightly around my hair, and I'm holding my helmet between my knees with my gloves inside.

My booted foot taps impatiently on the concrete. I'm waiting for Dwayne to bring my first Harley home. I see his truck curve around the corner near our house. A large black-and-white motorcycle hulks in the back of the truck.

I feel a wave of anxiety and nervousness at the sheer mass of it. Dwayne gets out of the truck and looks at me standing there, clutching my gloves in my hand. He kisses me on the forehead and pushes my helmet onto my head. "Hell, you're a Harley rider now. Go out there and kick some ass."

I help him roll the Harley down the ramp from the truck into the street. For the first time, I realize it is a police motorcycle—a Road King with hard saddlebags and a tall windshield on the large front fairing. The Road King displays the black-and-white color scheme of a police Harley-Davidson. The outline of the Mountain View police emblem it once wore peeks from beneath the white paint on the center of the gas tank. The buttons on the handlebars include ones for a siren and flashing lights. I push them experimentally. Dwayne laughs and tells me they're disconnected, so I won't be able to lead parades.

I swing my leg over the wide seat and swing both feet up on the wide footboards while Dwayne steadies the front. I perch high above the sidewalk. I put my left foot down, balancing the bulk of the Police Special against my leg. Dwayne squats down by me. He shows me how to work the heel and toe shifter of a Harley. I step down on my heel to move into higher gears and down on the front pedal to move into lower gears.

"Take her off the kickstand, baby." I push the kickstand back with my left foot. I am standing on my toes, since the motorcycle is too high for me to put my feet down flat. I look at Dwayne, and he nods.

I hit the starter button, and the motor rumbles to life. The motorcycle sways lightly beneath me like some strange beast when the vibration of the motor shakes it and me. I pull up on the shifter into first gear. I accelerate slightly and swing my feet up onto the footboards. The motorcycle surges forward.

I plan to ride through the parking lot of the school across the street on a test ride to see if I can control the heavier bike. I lean slightly left to turn into the driveway. The Harley leans with me. I wiggle my butt, and she sways slightly back and forth with me.

My Harley and I dance together through the parking lot. Wind rushes over the windshield and across my face. Strands of hair tickle the back of my neck as the wind lifts it. I accelerate and shift my way across the parking lot and back into the street.

I slow down in front of our garage and stick up my left hand. Dwayne slaps my palm in a high five and laughs out loud. I ride up and down the streets of our neighborhood for an hour. Each time I pass our garage, I see Dwayne sitting in a lawn chair in the doorway. He waves or gives me a thumbs-up as I roll by him.

Our weekly ritual becomes a Sunday ride. We cross the Golden Gate Bridge. We ride the Pacific Coast Highway from Pismo to San Francisco. We climb our way through Yosemite. I lead the way on the Police Special. He rides beside me on the right. Our motors growl together in a symphony.

A CLOSE CALL

On an early June morning one year after I get my motorcycle license, we are getting ready to ride to Elko, Nevada, for my first motorcycle rally. We will celebrate both my birthday and my first year of riding solo at the Elko Jamboree. The alarm rings at four, but we packed the bikes the night before.

I roll mine out of the garage, and I pull out the choke slightly and hit the starter. As it warms loudly in the dark, I put on chaps and my leather jacket. I tie my bandana around my hair and cinch on my half helmet. Dwayne does the same by his. I ease my right leg across the seat in front of my tour pack. We ride out of our neighborhood side by side.

As the sun rises in front of us, we begin our ride across the Sierra Nevada mountains. The moist warm wind pushes across my face. The smell of pines and sage fills my nose. The Police Special pulsates below me.

I am leaning into a sharp uphill corner when my front tire hits gravel. The Harley shudders beneath me, and I shift my weight to restore my balance on the bike. At the same moment, the rear tire skids sideways, small rocks flying in every direction. One pings off my helmet. My knees drag the pavement, the denim of my jeans shredding but saving my leg.

My motorcycle instructor Bill's voice echoes in my ear. *You don't have time for an oh shit moment on a motorcycle.* I act without thinking. Push in the opposite direction of the fall. Start shifting down. Do not grab the front brake. Tap the back one. I do all of that at the same time. The Harley pitches back to an erect stance but weaves back and forth at an increased rate of speed, because I am now on the downhill side of the mountain.

Taking a deep breath, I wrestle the handlebars to get the motorcycle back on a straight path again. But now the Harley and I are headed directly toward the edge of the road. Below the brink is nothing but a sheer drop. I hesitate a second to wonder if I should compress the front brake completely. The bike would instantly stop. I would fall off, but that might be a better option. In this brief moment of thinking, out of nowhere a short piece of concrete appears in front of my tire. The motorcycle hits the chunk with a lurch.

But it pushes me away from the edge. I have the Harley back in the center of the road. I am sitting up in the saddle, the bike not leaning beneath me now. I loosen the knots in my shoulders and swing my head a little to relax. Ahead I see another steep curve. I shift up a gear and roll the throttle to accelerate into the curve. My Harley and I swing through it without a pause.

Behind me, I hear Dwayne tap out a *beep beep beep* signal to congratulate me. Both of us need to stop and to recover. However, nothing but breakneck curves and lofty mountain roads wait for me. I can't stop until I'm through this part of the mountains. For the next thirty minutes, I shift and power my way over the rest of the twisty two-lane road until we reach the interstate.

I pull into the first gas station. As soon as I stop, I get off and walk with shaky legs to a nearby bench. I lean over my knees and wonder if I'm going to throw up as a wave of nausea hits me.

Dwayne parks by me with a squeal of tires on asphalt. He squats by the bench and rests his hand on my back, rubbing it gently. "That was scariest damn thing I've ever seen."

He takes a deep breath. "You accept the risk of riding when you're on two wheels. But it's a whole different thing when the biker is your wife and you're watching her start to plunge off a mountain."

He stands and pulls out his pack of cigarettes and taps the bottom repeatedly against the wall. One pops out, but he doesn't take it. He keeps clicking his lighter with one hand and beating the pack against the block wall rhythmically. "I've been riding Harleys forty years, and I've never seen anyone do what you just did." He lights his cigarette and laughs. "I think your mom must have been watching over you and threw that chunk of concrete there to save you."

I pull him down beside me and stretch out on the bench, my head on his knee. "I've never been so afraid in my life." I take a deep breath. "But I kinda feel proud of myself. I really can ride a bagger Harley."

We don't move. Cars and trucks drive in and out of the station. Trees bend back and forth in the light wind. The smell of his cigarette drifts across me. He strokes my hair.

Then I stand up and stretch the kinks out of my muscles. I wipe the sweat off my face with my bandana. Dwayne brings me a bottle of water from the cooler he has strapped onto his back fender.

I walk to my motorcycle and stand by it for a few minutes. Then I pull my helmet in place. "What are you waiting for? Your promised me a steak dinner and a margarita for my birthday." I swing my leg over the seat and look at him. I point to the shredded knee of my jeans. "You gotta buy me a new pair of jeans too."

He grins and shakes his head. "Crazy-ass biker."

Our engines roar to life in unison. We drop over the mountain into the flat desert on our way to Elko, separate but never more together.

MOTHERS

My stepdaughter, Jessica, and I experience our first real mother-daughter connection as we sit side by side in a Santa Cruz tattoo shop. Books of possible designs for our tattoos lie open in our laps. We take turns pointing out the ones we like to each other. I choose a small angel. I want something that will remind me of my mother, who had dozens of angels all over her tiny, cramped house. Jessica wants something with roses and crosses. Dwayne leans against the wall by us. He points to his faded tattoo with a Harley motor on his upper right arm. He warns us to make sure we want to live with it for the rest of our lives.

Then he laughs, "Hell, you know I love the idea of my girls getting tattoos together."

Jessica takes my hand. "My mom would never let me do this. She sure wouldn't be doing this with me."

I feel a moment of pride. Doubt quickly replaces the pride. I fear my newfound independence and confidence has warped my good sense as a mother.

Michael, who will do Jessica's tattoo, interrupts my second thoughts. He asks Jessica to work with him to sketch out what her tattoo will look like. He flips open the cover on a large notebook.

She describes the colors and elements she wants in hers. His pen flies over the page as she talks. As Dwayne and I watch, an intricate design of yellow roses—for Texas—and a Celtic cross in the center appears. Jessica looks at us and smiles. She follows him to his booth and sits sideways in the chair. He plops down on a rolling stool and pulls over his tray of tools. Soon the buzz of the needle fills the air.

Now it's my turn to meet with my tattoo artist, Damian. He and I stand on opposite sides of the front counter. I lean over his notebook. He flips to a new page. I show him the angel I have chosen. Like Jessica I start to tell him how I want it to look. I stop. Damian looks up from the notebook.

"You know, I don't think I want an angel."

"What picture really sticks in your mind?" he prompts me.

"Dragons." I don't know where that comes from, but I like the idea as soon as it comes out of my mouth. "I teach Beowulf every year. I want an English kind of dragon. With flames."

Damian laughs. "Good choice. See what you think of this." His pencil curves and corners on the page. A winged emerald dragon appears. Orange-and-red flames curl around his head. A forked tail spirals below him. The tattoo is much larger and more elaborate than my simple angel.

"I love it!" Then I hesitate. "I really want HD for Harley-Davidson on it somewhere."

"No problem." An ebony HD appears in the center of the flames.

We shake hands. I follow him back to his booth. Like Jessica I sit sideways on the vinyl chair covered with a white sheet and lean over a high table by it. Damian, on his stool behind me, swabs my right shoulder where I will put the tattoo. The cold alcohol tingles on my skin. He lays his sketch down on my shoulder after the alcohol dries. He outlines the dragon where it will be engraved.

He presses down hard with a special pen to create an outline for the actual tattoo.

Then he picks up the needle. A long electric cord snakes from it. He flips the switch. I hear the buzz of the needle before I feel it. At first I feel each pulsation of the needle as it penetrates my skin—a small electric tingle each time. Then, in a few minutes, I only feel a numbness and vibration.

Outside the large front window, Dwayne smokes and peers in at me with the bright streetlights behind him. He gives me a thumbs-up and grins. I lean my forehead on my arm and eventually doze off and on for the next two hours.

I wake with a start when a sharp pain shoots down my arm. The needle pauses. Damian lays his hand on my arm. He tells me he is rolling the ink into the dragon's wings to create a 3-D effect. This will also cause the color in the tattoo to last longer. I grit my teeth and nod, and he turns the needle back on.

I hear Dwayne's engineer boots thudding across the floor. He squats down by me. "You okay, baby?" I nod yes. Then he stands up and bends over my back to see the tattoo for the first time. "Goddamn, that sure ain't no little angel!"

He sinks back down on his heels. We look at each other and laugh. "I tell you, Mary Jane Black, you're a real biker now. You aren't that shy English teacher I met in Chili's anymore."

"I'm still an English teacher, just a biker one."

At three in the morning, Jessica and I walk out of the shop with our brand-new tattoos stinging on our bodies. Dwayne opens the door for each of us. We nod off to sleep as we drive the twisting road over Mount Madonna to our home in Morgan Hill.

I wake up the next morning to the smell of coffee. Dwayne hears me get up and brings me a cup. He carries a bottle of peroxide and cotton swabs. As I drink the hot coffee, he gently washes the new tattoo. He tapes on a new soft gauze. Then he kisses me good morning.

As I get ready for school, he goes into Jessica's room to wake her up. He will take care of her tattoo too. She has recently moved to California to live with us. Now she attends the high school where I teach. It has been a lot of firsts for both of us. Strangely, our tattoo adventure is the first time we feel like a family.

The bond we created in the tattoo parlor becomes strained over the new few weeks. Late at night we hear her voice murmuring in the dark while she talks to her mother. Each day we come home together after school. She slams the door behind her when she retreats to her room. She either ignores us or yells at us in unexpected angry outbursts. She doesn't want to go with us anymore on our weekend rides.

One day at lunch I am grading papers and working on lesson plans. As usual Jessica hides out in my room to eat her lunch and to avoid the other students. Now she sits hunched over a table at the back of the room. Her long pale blond hair hangs down and covers her face. She slowly pokes her food with a fork. I look up and watch her for a few minutes. I see her wipe away tears.

"Hey, are you okay?"

"I miss my friends back home."

I recommend trying to make some new friends. I know it is useless advice even as I give it.

"You just don't understand," she says defiantly. "I didn't think I'd miss home so much. Or my mom. You're nothing like her."

"I'm trying, Jess. I really am." I go to the table. I sit down and put my arm around her.

She pulls away. "She never tells me what to do. My mom said you control everything I do because you don't trust me." Her voice rises with each complaint.

I shake my head and say, "I don't expect anything from you that I didn't expect from Stephanie."

The bell stops us from continuing the conversation. At the end of the day she meets me at my car in the parking lot. We drive home in silence.

That night at dinner Jessica lays down her fork suddenly. "I have to tell you guys something. I don't want you to be mad." Dwayne and I look at her. We wonder what is coming next.

"I've been talking to Mom," she starts, "and she's coming next week to see me. I told her she can stay here. We're going to talk about my going home."

"Jess, why haven't you talked to me about this before?" Dwayne reaches out to take her hand.

"I just couldn't," she chokes out the words between tears.

Dwayne stands up and pushes back his chair. "Let's talk, Jessie Lane." They go out on the front porch.

For the next two hours, I read and listen to the creak of the rocking chairs on the front porch. I can't hear the words, just the sad melody of their voices floating through the open window.

The week quickly passes. Dwayne and Jessica pick her mom, Janice, up at the airport. For three days Jessica directs us as her California tour guides. We visit all of the places she likes. We do not talk about Jessica's staying with us or going home with her mom. I ask Dwayne if we should talk to Janice, and he says it's safer to let Janice decide when she wants to talk. He learned that the hard way when they were married.

One evening we return from a day in San Francisco. Dwayne opens the garage door for the car. Our Harleys gleam in the glare of the headlights.

Janice turns to look at me in the dim light. "I was so surprised to hear you ride a motorcycle. A Harley. That is hardly the behavior I expect from a teacher. I am not sure I would have agreed to let Jessica live here if I had known you were that sort of person. I expect such irresponsible behavior from Dwayne but not you. Next thing I know you'll be getting a tattoo."

"Get ready for my really bad example for Jessica, then. I got a tattoo a few weeks ago." The words are out before I can stop them.

"I'm getting my daughter out of your house." Janice swivels away from me and marches down the sidewalk to our house. The door slamming echoes in the dark night. We stare at each other in the glow of the streetlights.

Jessica pleads, "Don't tell Mom I got a tattoo too."

I assure her that it is her secret to tell. "How are you going to keep your mom from seeing your tattoo?"

"She never pays any attention to me. She just wants to make sure no one sees it and thinks she's a bad mother."

We stand in silence with the moths fluttering around the light above us.

Finally Dwayne lays his hand on her shoulder. "You're going back to Texas, aren't you?"

"I love you, Daddy. But I don't belong here. I'm not a California kind of girl. You guys don't need me. You and Mary have each other. Mom needs me. She has a ticket for me for a flight home."

He hugs her tightly. She turns to me. I hug her too. We clutch each other in a tight circle.

Two days later we drop Jessica and Janice off at the curb at the airport. Dwayne pulls out their suitcases from the trunk. A large box with Jessica's stuff will be mailed. The rest she has left behind. She says it will be there when she visits. We stand awkwardly in the foggy San Jose morning. We chat for a few uncomfortable minutes.

Around us people hug and say goodbye. Finally, Janice pulls up the handle of her wheeled suitcase and tells Jessica she'll meet her inside. She goes through the sliding doors. They silently glide closed behind her.

"Bye, Daddy and Mary," Jessica whispers. "I do love you." She leaves us, pulling her suitcase behind her. She disappears into the terminal.

Dwayne and I drive away. A family of two.

BIKER CHICK

I ease my new carburetor in place with my grease-stained hands. Dwayne leans against the workbench with coffee in one hand and guides me through the process with the other hand waving in the air. A Mikuni carburetor was my anniversary gift this year, and Dwayne promises me it will increase the speed of my motorcycle.

He told me when I started riding solo that there are two types of bikers: the ones who ride a bike at one hundred miles per hour and say, "Yes!" and the ones who ride at one hundred miles per hour and say, "Oh, hell, no!" I'm definitely a "yes" rider, living for the feeling of flying on two wheels down a highway.

A shadow falls across the concrete floor. We both look up and recognize the woman who lives next door. I stand up and wipe my hands on a towel. Dwayne walks across the floor to shake her hand. We both introduce ourselves.

She nods at both of us and tells us her name is Gail. She shoves her hands into the pockets of her navy-blue windbreaker. "I've been watching Mary riding her motorcycle." She chuckles. "I'm a little embarrassed to admit I peeked through the window when she rode that Harley through the school parking lot across the street."

I ease down my motorcycle on the stand and sit sideways on the seat with my legs stretched out in front of me. "Yeah, that was when Dwayne brought it home for the first time."

I gently pat the black gas tank with its ghost flames. "It looks a lot different than it did that day."

Gail clears her throat. "You may think I'm crazy, but I've decided I want to ride a motorcycle after watching you. What are you going to do with the Honda?" She points to my first motorcycle, the Honda Shadow, sitting in the corner.

Dwayne tells her we haven't thought about what to do with it yet.

I look at her and smile. "How about you buy it and we'll help you learn to ride?"

She walks over and stands by it. Following her across the concrete floor, I hand her the key and show her how to start it. "It needs to be in neutral when you turn the key to start. The Harley will start in any gear, but it leaps forward with you hanging on."

She turns the key, and the motor rumbles. "It sounds more like a Harley than a Honda."

"Yep, Harley parts and a new exhaust."

Gail and I agree on a price, and she tells me she'll bring me a check the next day. We shake hands on the deal.

Dwayne rolls it down the sidewalk to her garage for her. She stands and stares at it as we walk away with a wave.

He throws his arm over my shoulders and laughs. "You just sold your first motorcycle."

Over the next three weeks, we watch her roll the Honda out of the garage. She sits on the seat and walks it flat-footed down the driveway. Dwayne and I help her learn about shifting and accelerating. Often he clasps the front of it while she tries to put her feet up on the pegs and balance her weight. She struggles with this balancing act. She never starts the motor while trying to keep it upright.

One afternoon we hold our breath as she starts the motor, swings her feet up on the pegs, and rolls the throttle forward in one smooth motion. Her foot pulls up on the gear shifter. The motorcycle lurches forward, but it stays upright when she squeals out of the parking lot. She pumps a fist in the air as she rolls down the street. We wave and shout encouragement when she passes our garage.

Every Saturday morning after that triumphant first ride, Gail and I meet on the street between our houses after Dwayne has ridden off to work at the Harley dealership. We pick a spot on the map—sometimes near us and sometimes a hundred miles or more away. Side by side we ride to our chosen destination. We park our motorcycles and eat lunch. We laugh about helmet hair and sweaty bras on hot days. I have found my first woman rider friend.

We learn that women motorcycle riders experience riding differently than men. I know if my Harley rolls against a speed bump while I'm backing out of a parking space, it will take an almost impossible burst of strength to push its 850 pounds of mass over it. It is clearly not a graceful act. Doing this in front of a crowd of men makes it especially difficult. One gentleman usually offers to help. This always makes me unreasonably angry.

One Saturday afternoon we sit in a booth at the Crazy Horse Diner in King City. The remains of our hamburgers on our plates have been pushed into a pile in the middle of the chrome-and-Formica table. Gail and I sit across from each other with mugs of coffee. Beside the dirty plates we've rolled out a map. We are trying to find a blue-marked road to take home. Blue roads are two lanes with little traffic and peaceful country on both sides. On a motorcycle you can feel the warm wind brushing through the tall golden grass. You can smell the cough-drop-scented eucalyptus trees.

We finally decide on one. I go find the pay phone to call Dwayne at San Jose Harley to let him know where we are and when I'll be home. I hear him yell out my location to his cowork-ers. He tells me all of them love to know where his old lady has ridden to on Saturdays.

I walk back to the table just as Gail returns from the restroom. She shows me a crumpled piece of paper. "I think we should con-tact this women's biker group to ride with."

I take the paper and read it. *Eagle Riders of Northern Califor-nia. An All-Woman Riding Club.* Under this title is a blurry picture of a woman on a large motorcycle, the words *Contact Carolyn Clark*, and a phone number.

Gail pulls the paper out of my hand. I agree it's time we rode with a group. We both admit it's a little scary to consider riding in the middle of a group of strangers. I've only ridden with her and Dwayne.

"Dwayne always says a turtle never gets anywhere until it sticks out its neck. So let's stick out our necks and give it a try!"

We walk outside and start to get dressed for the ride home. My Harley stutters as it warms. I swing my leg over the seat and yell to Gail over the noise of our engines. "I'll call this Carolyn Clark to see if we can meet her and the group."

We pick up our feet and roll out of the diner parking lot. The sun falls down over the mountains as we ride north in the cooling wind to Morgan Hill and home.

Early the next Saturday morning we sit outside a coffee shop in Hollister. Carolyn told me on the phone she would meet us there. I could hear her take a deep breath into the phone before she said, "There's really not a group of women yet. You two will be the first ones."

We told each other goodbye, and I heard her say we would meet at the coffee shop in Hollister and then ride over Pacheco Pass to a bar she knows over the mountains in Los Banos. Nei-ther Gail nor I have ever ridden the steep mountain pass near our houses. We argued during the week about whether we should cancel or just admit we can't ride over Pacheco.

Now I lean back in the metal chair outside the coffee shop. Beside me Gail hunches over the table with her hands wrapped around her paper coffee cup. Her booted foot taps against the concrete under the table. She turns and looks at me and opens her mouth to speak.

"Don't even say we can't ride over Pacheco Pass. Let's just wait until we meet this Carolyn and then decide." I sip my hot coffee and try not to burn my tongue.

A shotgun of sound fills the air. An enormous bright purple motorcycle swings with ease into the parking lot. The woman on the seat towers above the large windshield and wears a full helmet and studded leather gloves on the controls, making her seem more machinelike than human. We can see she also wears full black leathers from her neck to her booted feet. She pushes the tall heavy motorcycle back with ease against the curb next to our bikes.

Gail looks at me. "Do you think that's her?"

I squint in the bright sun. "It has to be." I try to find a way to describe the person striding across the lot toward us. "She is not very, well, feminine."

"You mean no boobs or hips." Gail sums it up.

The woman, and it is a woman, pulls off her helmet when she reaches our table. Her short spiky auburn hair springs up. Her tanned brown face wrinkles as she smiles at us. Her emerald green eyes examine us as we stand there speechless.

She peels off her gloves. Her wide hand grasps mine, and she pumps it up and down. "I'm Carolyn Clark. Just call me C.C. Everyone does." She turns to Gail and slaps her on the shoulder. Gail sways a little from the force.

We drop down in our chairs. C.C. drags over a chair from

another table. She wedges herself into it. She fires off a series of questions at us. We try to answer them with the history of our riding. The history is brief for me and Gail compared to C.C.'s story. She started riding dirt bikes at seven and rode in flat track races at twelve.

C.C. stands up and pushes her chair back against the wall with a bang. "Let's hit the road." She marches off the patio toward our motorcycles.

Gail and I stand up and stare at each other. I straighten my shoulders, wrap my bandana around my hair, and pick up my helmet.

Gail reaches out and grabs my arm. "Are you actually going to follow that woman over a mountain pass on a motorcycle?"

I wave back at C.C. as she motions with her arm to join her. "I sure as hell am not going to tell her I don't think I can do it." I buckle on my helmet. "You know, the funny thing is she kind of makes me think I can. Her confidence is contagious."

I meet C.C. at the motorcycles, looking at hers for the first time up close. It is a Honda Valkyrie, a massive machine with a bulky chrome motor that bulges out of the frame. I watch in awe when she swings effortlessly onto the seat. She snaps up the kickstand and balances the bulk of the bike against her right leg. Without even looking to see if Gail and I are ready, her Valkyrie bolts with a screech of her back tire out of the parking space.

Both Gail and I, with our legs frozen in the motion of sliding over our seats, watch her swerve and glide out of the lot with a fluid movement, as if she were on one of her dirt bikes and not a motorcycle with a six-speed engine resembling a car motor.

I catch up with her and stay on the right side. Gail pulls out behind me. She aligns herself to my left. I watch the purple Honda speed down the highway white line ahead of me. I accelerate to keep up with C.C. I hear Gail's smaller Honda engine whine, struggling to keep up.

The next thirty minutes pass in a blur. I lean and shift into corners. The Valkyrie's red brake lights blinks on and off as it swings around the sharp bends in the road. I increase my speed and veer my Harley to one side and then another, following in C.C.'s path. When I lean into the curves, the footboards on my Road King spark against the pavement. I climb higher and higher over the mountains on my motorcycle, and I can see the sides of cars inches away, passing me going down the sloping road. I feel the hot wind of their exhaust.

Suddenly, the Road King surges forward, and we begin to descend the mountain. Now I need to tap my brake gently with my foot to slow the motorcycle down. I resist the urge to grab the front brake lever. I gently pull the clutch and tap down on the shifter to decrease my speed. I bob and weave around corners. The reservoir on my right glints in the sunshine. I don't risk looking at it.

The road straightens. We slow down, and I can now look at the sun-browned hills around me. I push myself back slightly from the handlebars. My neck aches from leaning over them. I flex my left hand, which has been furiously grabbing and releasing the clutch to shift.

A horn beeps on my left side. I glance over at Gail, who has ridden up beside me. She waves her left hand wildly in the air. "Whoopee!"

Sharing her celebration, I pump my fist in the air.

We throttle forward with a burst of speed. We keep C.C. on her Valkyrie in sight as we roll on down the highway.

My legs almost buckle under me when we get to the bar in Los Banos, and I slither off my seat. Gail and I stare at each other across our bikes and say at the same time, "I can't fucking believe I did that."

Over the next few weeks, no one else joins C.C.'s biker group, but the three of us become a fearless trio of female riders. Gail and

C.C. soon become partners and lovers, and Gail moves to Hollister to live with her, no longer my next-door neighbor.

Often on our regular rides, we follow C.C. without question when she turns off the freeway onto a narrow gravelly road that disappears at the top of a steep peak. C.C., like Dwayne, believes being a woman doesn't mean you can't do any damn thing you want to do on a motorcycle.

Several months later, the sun glints off the steel of the Bay Bridge when the group of a hundred women on motorcycles ride side by side across it. My rearview mirror reflects the San Francisco skyline behind me. C.C.'s brake lights flicker off and on in front of me as she controls her speed to match the bike in front of her. She, Gail, and I are riding by choice at the back of the pack.

I glance to my right and watch Gail move up beside me. She clutches her handlebars. She stares straight ahead and doesn't look at me. Her nervousness about riding with such a large group of women made us to decide to ride behind everyone.

Now the Bay shines indigo in the afternoon sun. The heat from it warms my back in its leather vest. I lean back against the backrest Dwayne made for me and prop one boot up on my highway bars on the front wheel. I take a moment to enjoy the warmth after a foggy start.

Most of the motorcycles in this motorcycle club are Harleys. I met a couple of the women at San Jose Harley, where I was leaning against the parts counter talking to Dwayne. They asked me to join them on this motorcycle run. Their club is known as the Devil Dolls, the only all-female riding club associated with the Hell's Angels. Most of them ride Sportsters, a Harley that outlaw bikers believe women can handle. Only a few ride large Harleys like my Road King. I know they invited me because they were curious about a woman on a Road King with a husband who thought she could and should ride one.

Now I have arrived with two gay women on Hondas, and C.C., with her size and confidence, always draws attention. Suddenly a blast of reverberation rattles through the bridge. All bikers love to roll their throttle forward to create a boom of noise on bridges and in tunnels. I roll my throttle forward while holding the brake, adding my roar to theirs. People in cars on our left wave and take pictures.

I survey the long stream of women on motorcycles ahead of me and think how far I've come since I married Dwayne five years ago. He told me I would make a million new friends when I rode a Harley. I thought they'd be Dwayne's biker friends, but now I have my own circle of motorcycle friends.

Ahead of me I see someone near the front stick their left hand in the air. They swing it back and forth to tell us we are turning left. The gesture is repeated down the line of motorcycles. Two by two the riders and motorcycles lean through the turn while one woman on a motorcycle stops traffic at a stop sign. The smooth movement of the women resembles a snake undulating through the corner until we are all on the freeway. The woman stopping traffic blasts by us on the left to take her place again at the head of the line.

We ride on freeways and side roads until we come to a ramshackle restaurant and bar at the edge of a muddy river. The wooden building leans slightly to the left. Paint peels off in strips. With precision we park and back up against the curbs on both sides of the narrow paved road. Some women pull into the parking lot of the church across the street.

Gail and I push ourselves off our motorcycles. C.C. joins us. She jerks off her bandana, and her hair springs up into its usual bristly form. She takes Gail's hand and walks toward the bar.

The darkness inside the bar makes us blink after the glare of the sun. Tangled strands of hair hang down in my eyes. I pull them back into a ponytail. I haven't worn a head wrap under my helmet today, so my hair has been whipped and tangled by the wind.

The three of us maneuver our way through the crowd of women until we elbow our way up to the scarred wooden bar. C.C. grabs the harried bartender by the elbow and orders three beers. The noise of the raised voices and a heavy metal song on the jukebox deafen us. We don't try to talk. We just stand and watch the crowd.

After an hour, we are tired of watching and are ready to move on. We empty our beer bottles and decide to ride south to the Hell's Angels party in Oakland, which follows the motorcycle ride. I find one of the women I know and tell her we'll meet her there. She tells me the men are already there and waiting for us. We swing out of the parking lot and ride in a line down the busy city street.

Once we're on the freeway, C.C. shoots into the traffic. I watch her weave through the heavy traffic. I shadow her and hope Gail is close behind us. In traffic like this you are on your own. At times I need to ride the white line and split lanes down the middle of the freeway between the stopped cars.

Eventually, we pull off the freeway onto a long straight stretch of empty road across the rolling brown hills. C.C. accelerates rapidly. I grab my throttle and speed up beside her. I check the speedometer and see I'm going ninety miles per hour.

Then I accelerate and move ahead of her. The wind slams into my face. My helmet skates back on my hair from the force. I watch the needle on the speedometer jump past one hundred. I release the throttle and feel my Harley slow down beneath me. My heart bangs against my ribs, and I shove my helmet back in place. I pat my gas tank with appreciation for the ride.

C.C. rides up beside me and shouts, "Felt fucking good, didn't it?"

I grin at her with a thumbs-up.

Soon we're pulling into the parking lot of a steel-sided warehouse. Hundreds of newly washed Harleys, shimmering in the setting sun, stand in regimented rows all around us. We find a place for us to park and turn off our engines. I can hear the music drumming inside of the building. Large groups of men in leather vests with the Hell's Angel skull and wing patches stand around with beers in their hands.

I search for Dwayne in the crowd. He was riding here with our friend Desmond—the owner of Motor Shop, where we take our scooters for repairs, and a Hell's Angel himself—and some of Dwayne's customers and friends from the Harley shop. Finally, I see him wave from where he's leaning against a truck parked against the building. I wave back. We weave our way around the bikes and bikers between us until we meet.

We hug each other, and our sun-warmed leather vests press together with a sticky sound. "How was it, baby?" He rubs his whiskered cheek against mine.

"The ride was sort of boring. I did get to race C.C. a little."

He leans back and raises his eyebrows to ask for more details.

I lay my hand on top of my flattened hair. "I found out my helmet slides back at ninety miles per hour."

Dwayne breaks an ironclad biker rule and leans against someone else's windshield when he bends over laughing. "My teacher wife and now a badass biker. I love you more now than I did on that day in Eureka Springs when we got married."

He grabs me and pulls me closer. "I'm damn proud of you, Mary Jane. Some assholes want their wife to stay the same, but your changing only made you a better wife. And riding buddy."

I lock my arms around his waist. "All because of you, sweetie."

We wade through the crowd to find a beer. Two thirsty bikers who happen to be married to each other.

BROKEN WING

As I round a corner on my Road King, a woman on a Honda Goldwing slams into me. I feel a bone-shaking thud on my left leg. I look down at my boot and see the footboard curled around it like a fist. My motorcycle shudders beneath me. I focus on trying to keep it upright and to stop it. I fail at both.

I see the front wheel lift off the pavement, preparing to somersault backward. I release the handlebars. I swing my left leg over the gas tank, and I dive onto the asphalt below me. I carefully keep myself upright by placing my hands palms down onto the rough surface, feeling the tar and gravel dig into my fingertips. I finally glide to a stop and see my fractured Harley lying on its side to my left.

I hear Dwayne yelling my name before I see him. He drops to his knees by me. Tears run down his face and drip into his mustache. "Mary. Baby." His voice cracks on the words. A man I've never seen at a loss for words can't find any.

I shout at him. "Goddamn it. What the hell just happened?"

He starts to respond, but I interrupt him. "You need to get my motorcycle off the road. Then you can help me get up. I don't think I can stand."

Around us we hear other motorcycles shutting off, and we see riders working to clear the road before more cars on the road appear. A woman wearing a Honda jacket squats down by us and asks if she can help. I ask her to help Dwayne get my bike off the road and to find out if the other rider is okay.

Dwayne returns in a few minutes and scoops me up in his strong arms. He leans his forehead against mine and fiercely whispers, "Don't you fucking die on me."

He carries me to the side of the road and sits me down in the warm grass. He helps me take off my helmet and then the bandana beneath it. The wind lifts my sweaty hair and dries the blood on it into a stiff brown mass I can feel with my fingers. Dwayne dabs at a cut on my cheek with his bandana. He grips my knee with his other hand. We both stare at my left foot, which hangs at a strange angle.

"Can you move it?" He lays a hand on my left knee.

I try to move my foot upright. A stab of pain shoots up my leg. It doesn't move. I tell Dwayne he has to take the boot off. He tries to unlace it, but I grab his hand to stop him. A wave of dizziness hits me. My foot throbs with pain.

He takes out his pocket knife and looks at me. I nod. He saws raggedly through the back of the boot with the sharp knife and then slips it off my foot. The once white sock glistens red in the sun. We agree a doctor will have to remove that.

Suddenly a large man in a bright blue riding suit marches up to us. "You fucking hit my wife."

I feel Dwayne tense beside me. He stands up. "Your fucking wife hit mine," he replies softly. When Dwayne is the angriest, he becomes very quiet first. He is seldom angry these days, but I know he will always protect me.

"Hey, both of you! Let's get the two of us to a hospital, and we'll worry about blame later." My teacher's voice commands the situation.

Suddenly we hear the *whump whump* sound of a helicopter landing. We watch one with a red cross on the side land in a nearby field. The rotor wind whips the tall grass. The paramedics jump out before the motor shuts off.

For the first time, I notice the other rider sitting near a tree to my right. The woman sits and leans slightly against the trunk of the tree. She's still fully dressed in her riding leathers. The paramedics go to her. I watch them talk. She waves her hands wildly in the air. Her husband turns away from us suddenly and rushes to join them.

Soon one of the medics walks away and approaches us. The young man in his blue EMS shirt crouches down by me. He gently lifts my left foot. I bite my lip to keep from screaming. Dwayne clutches my hand tightly. Then the medic wraps a tan elastic bandage around my foot and straps it into a splint.

I feel the nerves and bones protesting the stiff support. Waves of nausea sweep over me. Beads of sweat pop out on my forehead, and Dwayne wipes them away with a gentle hand.

The young man kneels in front of me. "We can only take one of you in the helicopter. You're the most critically injured, but the other couple is threatening a lawsuit if we don't take her."

Dwayne starts to answer. I stop him by putting my hand on his arm. "Take her. I'm sure an ambulance and a wrecker are coming soon?"

He assures me they are. He runs back to his partner. They roll a stretcher to the woman and lift her into the helicopter. The rush of the wind pushes across us as they lift and leave.

Twenty minutes later an ambulance arrives with a rush of red lights and sirens. Earlier I watched the wrecked motorcycles being boosted onto a trailer. Now it's my turn to make my way to an emergency room. Dwayne follows us on his motorcycle. I hear the rumble behind us beneath the shrill siren.

In the emergency room, people in a variety of colored scrubs rush around silently. Curtains around the beds fly open.

Dwayne sits perched on the side of my bed, rubbing my arm, then my thigh. He strokes my hair. Every five minutes he asks, "Are you okay, baby?"

Suddenly he stands and leans over me in the bed. "You know what this whole thing made me realize?"

I shake my head no. I lay my hand over his on my stomach. The joined hands warm me through the thin sheet.

"I have to die first. I watched you come off that motorcycle and hit the road and knew I couldn't live if you had been killed." He leans closer to me. "Don't you leave me alone. Promise."

"I'm never going to leave you." I try to smile. My cheek aches as the edges of the cut break open again with the effort. "We've got to die together, because I couldn't live without you either."

A doctor and a nurse interrupt our talk. I am sent down for x-rays and tests. When I return, Dwayne and I look in amazement at the x-rays on the screen, and the doctor taps them with his pencil. Fragments of bones in my toes gleam white against the black background in the glare of the light. They look like pieces of a jumbled and scattered jigsaw puzzle.

"Every toe is crushed," the doctor pronounces. "In fact, the whole foot is shattered. The good news is we can reassemble your foot and hold it in place with a cast. You may need surgery." He pauses. "You know, sometimes injuries like this require amputation. Somehow your foot has maintained enough integrity to require only a cast."

"She rides a big Harley. The footboard wrapped around her foot and protected it. She's tough." He strokes my hair with one hand.

Soon they bind my shattered foot into a bulky white plaster cast. My foot tingles and throbs beneath the surface. A plastic surgeon wearing glasses with a magnifying glass extension sews the cut under my right eye from my broken sunglasses. He assures me when it heals, no one will even see it.

During my x-rays, Dwayne rushed home on his motorcycle and returned with our car. Someone pushes me outside now in my wheelchair. The darkness around us is split by the bright lights outside the hospital. Dwayne takes both of my hands and pulls me up. I slide into the passenger seat. He swings my legs into the car. We drive home, his right hand on my knee all the way.

The next morning, we go to the motorcycle shop where my Harley was taken after the accident. The owner and our friend, Desmond, along with his mechanic Mike follow us as Dwayne wheels me in my wheelchair into the workshop. My motorcycle sits on a lift in the center of the floor. The front wheel bends drunkenly toward the floor. Raw metal shines through the gouges and scrapes on the paint. Handlebars twist sharply at an awkward angle.

Dwayne and Desmond take turns pointing out the damage with admiration for my getting off it alive. I feel tears welling. "Damn it, I love my Police Special. I feel like you two are talking about my injured baby."

Mike looks at me. "Yeah, they just don't understand. If it were my knucklehead, I'd be sobbing out loud." He pats my shoulder in sympathy.

Dwayne assures me this just means I get a new Harley, because the insurance company will total it.

I put my hand up to stop him. "I don't want a new one. Can't you fix mine?"

Desmond and he exchange looks. They shake their heads at my stubbornness and say they can't. They take turns telling me about how they'll fix up my new Road King to make it mine too.

Dwayne lays his hand on mine where it clutches the

wheelchair arm. "Hell, we can get you another Police Special Harley if you want."

We drive home in silence. The next few weeks I spend the weekdays teaching in a wheelchair and then on crutches. On weekends we visit Harley shops to look at new Road Kings. Eventually the cast is removed, and I wear a stiff black walking boot.

When the doctor tells me I won't be able to ride for a year after surgery to repair the nerve damage, I refuse it. Dwayne and I have intense conversations about my riding again and the possibility of another accident. I remind him he always told me I made my own decisions.

I practice walking without a limp. I sit on Dwayne's motorcycle and push back the kickstand to get used to doing it with my healing foot. I practice shifting the weight from my tingling left foot to my right in an easy motion. He always watches me from a distance when I am on the Harley. But he keeps quiet.

One Saturday morning I sit in a rocking chair on the front porch with my foot in its plastic walking boot propped on a wooden chair. Dwayne has ridden off to work after he brought me my coffee and settled me into the chair. I can walk without help now, but he still wants to be sure I'm okay before he leaves.

Suddenly I hear the pulsating sound of Harley motors approaching. As I watch, I see Desmond, Mike, and Dwayne ride up and back each bike against the curb. I squint and peer into the morning sun at the motorcycle Dwayne parks. It looks just like my wrecked one. I stand up quickly. I balance myself by placing my hand on the railing. Then I walk stiffly down the sidewalk to meet them.

The three of them stand facing me with their helmets in their hands. All three wear broad smiles on their faces. Dwayne waves his hand toward the motorcycle he parked. "Are you surprised, baby?"

"What the . . ." I stammer. I stand by my resurrected Police Special. Its black paint gleams again in the California sunshine. The white of the ghost flames beneath the paint flickers again. "How did you do this?"

Desmond explains they thoroughly checked the frame to make sure it wasn't twisted. "We didn't want no death wobble."

Then he tells me that Dwayne enlisted their help to rebuild the motorcycle I loved. That explains the large number of over-time hours Dwayne has been working.

I wrap my hand around the left grip of the handlebars and lift my right leg. My left leg protests as my weight balances on the mending foot. I push my leg over the shiny black leather seat. I sit quietly on my rebuilt Harley and clench the grips tightly.

"We ain't done yet." I turn to look at Dwayne. He opens up one saddle bag with a snap. He pulls out my black leather vest. He hands it to me. "Look at the back, baby."

I clutch the soft leather in my hands and stare at the large Harley-Davidson bar and shield symbol with an eagle patch newly sewn on the back. A few snowy feathers drop from the outstretched amber-and-gold wings of the eagle. I rub my fingers over the silky fabric of the patch. I look at Dwayne.

"It's a broken wing patch. When you have an accident and an arm or leg is injured, it's traditional to wear it on your vest. You're one of the broken wing club members now."

I reach out my left hand, and he takes it. Desmond and Mike take turns slapping the palm of my right hand in celebration. We plan my first ride on the motorcycle in a few weeks, and I will wear my broken wing vest. I am back on the road again.

THE BREADWINNER

My mentor professor slips my blue-and-white-striped hood over my head with its silky fabric lying against my neck. I move forward on the stage, and behind me, my two teacher friends Thomasine and Stephanie also receive their Master's hoods from him. They join me, and we walk together down our row of seats. We turn to search the crowd for our husbands.

There in the front row of the bleachers I find Dwayne, snapping pictures and waving. Across the grass of the football field, I hear his shouts. "Whoop! Gig 'em." The Texas A&M Aggie chant of victory.

I wave back and give him a thumbs-up. A flash of memory comes to me. When I graduated with my undergraduate degree, I invited my mom. Tom stood by her with his arms crossed and a scowl on his face. He refused to go to dinner and told her to go home when we left the ceremony.

Today I smile as I watch Dwayne point me out to people sitting near him. I know he's telling them about his wife who just got a graduate degree in educational leadership.

I push my way through the crowd, keeping my eyes on him as he weaves his way toward me. He grabs me when I get close to him, and he rubs his cheek against mine, his mustache tickling my cheek. As he sings "My Girl" in my ear, we sway and shuffle in a celebration dance.

We're joined by Thomasine and Stephanie and their husbands. We pose for photographs in our robes with the hoods dangling down our backs.

Back in the parking lot, I pull off my graduation garments and fold them in my saddlebag. Under them, I've worn jeans and a Harley T-shirt. We rode our motorcycles to the graduation. Now I sit sideways on my seat and put on my boots.

As I get dressed for riding home, Dwayne trades out his polished cowboy boots for his battered engineer boots. "My master wife! I always knew you could do anything you wanted to."

I lean over his seat and kiss him. "You put up with me being gone a lot working and going to class."

"I always want you to do whatever makes you happy."

For lunch, we're meeting Dwayne's friend James, who worked with him at San Jose Harley until he quit to take a job at a custom motorcycle shop. He often joins us on Sunday rides. As we sit side by side in a booth, we watch him come in the front door.

He sits down and reaches across the table to shake my hand in congratulations. "Damn, girl, I always knew Dwayne had a smart wife."

Dwayne drapes his arm across my shoulders. "I tell you, James, you gotta go to Missouri and get you a teacher for a wife."

The two of them tell stories about customers they deal with each day, from Hell's Angels to orthodontists. They both agree the orthodontists are worse. Dwayne tells us about a group of doctors who bought chaps and jackets for Sturgis and then drove their cars over them in the driveway to make them look weathered. "They didn't want to have to ride all the way to North Dakota, so they trailered their scooters."

Finally, the waitress picks up our dirty dishes and drops the ticket on the table. James reaches for it and says it's his gift to me. "Hey, man, Don from the Harley shop said you quit last week. What are you going to do?"

I move away from Dwayne and turn to look at him. "You're quitting the Harley shop?"

He doesn't look at me but keeps his eyes on James. "Yeah, it ain't been the same since Dennis left to take that job in Hollywood."

On the ride home, I think about how he quit his job at the Harley dealership in Texas, which ended up precipitating our move to California. That job lasted three years, and now he's been working at San Jose Harley four years. I know we'll have to talk about his making the decision without me.

In the kitchen I pour us glasses of iced tea and sit at the table. Dwayne pulls out a chair, plopping down in it. He moves his glass in circles on the table, the condensation on the glass making watery streaks on the wood. He concentrates on the glass without talking.

I put my hand on his wrist and stop the movement of the glass. "We've got to talk about your job, you know."

He reaches in his pocket and pulls out his cigarettes, hesitating before tapping one out.

I get our one ash tray out of the cabinet and put it in front of him. He usually smokes outside or in the garage. He thanks me, since he knows I hate the smell of tobacco in the house. When I was a child with a smoker as a mother, I lived in a smoke-filled house with the tang of nicotine choking me and stinking my clothes.

He lights his cigarette and smokes without talking for a few minutes. "You know I always work a job like I own the business. But I don't take anyone's shit."

"You always seemed to love your work at San Jose Harley." I

run my finger down my chilled glass and watch him, his face in the shadows of the bright sunlight behind him.

"I did until Dennis left. I was supposed to be parts manager in his place."

I nod. He continues, "Then they hired Richard. That son of a bitch rides my ass all day long."

"You quit?"

"Yeah, we had a blowup last week, and I quit before I kicked his ass."

"Why didn't you tell me?"

He sits up straight in the hard chair. "I had to figure out what I was going to do next to bring in money."

I remember all of the ways he's made money over the years. One time I came home to find someone painting our house, even though we had no money to pay for it. Dwayne told me he'd rebuilt the man's Harley engine in exchange for his painting our house before we sold it.

Now he gets up from the table and brings a short stack of photographs to the table. He flips them on the table one at a time. "This here's a '57 Chevy John King bought last week. He's going to pay me to rebuild it."

He grabs his sketch pad and draws how he's going to restore the car's exterior. He tells me John is going to pay him $10,000. "You see, baby, I'll be bringing in money, just not a regular paycheck."

I take his hand. "I was just worried you didn't talk to me. We always have to be honest with each other."

"I sometimes forget you're not like my other wives. You love me just the way I am."

A few hours later, I'm standing in my principal Nancy's back-yard with a margarita in my hand. She has presented the three of us who've just completed our graduate degree with a toast. Now we're all relaxing with drinks and engaging in party small talk. The crowd bumping into each other represents the dissimilar groups that make up my friends. Teachers and administrators in Bermuda shorts and wrinkled cotton shirts chat with bikers in leather vests and scuffed boots, with tattoos covering the flesh turning pink in the hot afternoon sun.

In the corner of the yard, Dwayne holds a Corona in one hand, with his other hand gesturing while he tells a story. The circle of people around him laugh. I know he's probably telling an anecdote about one of our motorcycle trips. During the two years since my motorcycle accident, we've gone on several long-distance road trips. Las Vegas Bike Fest. Hollister Rally. Arizona Bike Week. Loughlin River Run. And home to Texas every July for his mother's birthday.

A short blond woman with her hair tucked under a pink bandana joins me. We stand and observe his storytelling for a few moments. She finally says, "He's quite a guy, your husband. We all love him."

"Yeah, it was love at first sight for me."

We move back a few steps to stand under the shade of the deck awning. She sips her beer and asks, "How long you two been married?"

"Seven years next month." I swirl my frozen margarita in its glass.

"No shit. I thought it was at least twenty years. You two seem so connected . . . like you spent your whole lives together."

I stare at my husband across the narrow yard, and my heart races the way it did in Chili's years ago seeing him for the first time on a blind date. He feels my eyes on him and looks up at me. We smile at each other across the crowd.

I make my way through the crowd and join him. He is talking about the time we rode home from Texas and hit a strong headwind outside Palm Springs. I stand and listen, adding details when he asks for them.

Skimming my hand down his back, I tuck my hand in the back of his belt. He shifts his weight until he leans against me. One of the women I work with asks me if I'm going to teach senior English again next year. Our motorcycle friends drift away as the talk shifts to school and students.

The sound of motorcycle motors interrupts us. We walk to the driveway to watch C.C. and Gail shut down their motors, restoring silence to the neighborhood. C.C. lifts me off the ground when she hugs me. The four of us go to the backyard and join the party.

At one point near the end of the evening, Nancy finds me in the kitchen, where I'm helping clean up. We move into the living room, where the noise from the backyard is more muted.

I drop onto the couch, and she slumps in the chair by me. "I wanted to talk to you about what your plans are now."

I lean forward. "I enjoyed being a literacy coach last year, so no immediate plans to find another job."

She hesitates and then says, "I'd like you to consider using that new administrator's certificate."

"I've never thought of myself as anything but a teacher."

"You'd be a hell of a principal." She says she'll be wanting an assistant principal in a couple of years, so I should think about it.

I do think about it on the ride home after all of the goodbyes and congratulations are finished.

Later that night, we are sitting in bed watching Loony Tunes, my head on Dwayne's shoulder. I sit up and mute the television. "How would you feel about me becoming an administrator? A vice principal."

He turns to me. "Is that something you'd want to do?"

"I think so." I stop and say, "I'd make a lot more money as an assistant principal. Nancy said it'd be a couple of years before a job opens here, but I'd like to try to find one now."

"I may be an old redneck, but I've got no problems being married to a woman with money." He grins at me. "You can be the breadwinner, baby."

We switch off the lamp, and I talk in the dark about the job of leading a school. The long hours. My being busy in the summer.

He assures me all he wants is for me to do what I want.

Over the next few weeks, I look online for administrator jobs, and after an interview, I'm finally offered one in the Central Valley near Modesto. We ride over the hills into the dry and hot valley one Sunday, and we look at the high school where I'll be working. We get a newspaper and sit at Starbucks, looking through the classified section for houses to rent. Dwayne reminds me it has to have a garage, the bigger the better. He'll work on cars and motorcycles at home as his full-time job.

I find the house with the large garage on the day I sign my contract. I call Dwayne, and he says he's good with me making the decision. "You're the boss, baby."

We move on a sweltering July day, and soon all of our belongings are unloaded in our new home. It will take Dwayne another week to bring all of his tools and stuff out of his old garage.

Before schools starts, Stephanie comes for a visit to see our new house. She rides behind Dwayne for a trip to Lake Tahoe. That night over dinner she tells us she's leaving John and moving into an apartment.

I lay my hand on hers. "We're here if you need us."

One day in the fall I come home from my new job to find an unfamiliar motorcycle in the garage. I drop my purse on the patio table and walk to the separate workshop. I can hear the welder buzzing inside the building. I step into the door and wait until he sees me. He's bent over a car fender and shaping the edge into a smooth roll of steel. He looks up and turns off the welder.

"Hey, where'd you get the new Harley in the garage?" I ask as I lean against the workbench.

"I got it from Desmond. It's a '49 panhead. Always wanted one." He pulls off his welding helmet.

"Are you selling it for him?"

"No, I bought it with the money I got from John for rebuilding his Chevy." He pushes the welder against the wall.

"All of it?" I move to stand beside him.

"Yeah, but I'm going to make a lot of money on this scooter." He describes how much panheads are selling for and how he's going to fix it up.

I cut his talk short. "I thought we were going to save that money for a down payment on a house."

He promises me he'll get it sold in a month. We shake hands on the deal, and Dwayne locks the workshop door behind us.

The weeks dash by. I spend my days dealing with student discipline and an endless schedule of meetings. Dwayne spends his restructuring the panhead. The month deadline for selling it passes. He puts it on eBay and waits for a response.

I force myself not to ask about it or if he's sold it yet.

Finally, I come home six months later to find the panhead gone. When I walk in the back door, I see Dwayne sitting at the kitchen table with a stack of forms in front of him. "What happened to the panhead?"

"I took it back to Desmond at Motor Shop. He gave me my money back and a little extra for upgrading the engine."

"What are those?" I gesture at the stack of papers in front of him.

"Insurance for my new job." He reaches down and picks up something from a chair seat. He tosses it to me.

I hold it up. It's a shirt. On the back it says *Mitchell Modesto Harley-Davidson.* The name tag on the front pocket says *Dwayne Black.* "A new job, huh?"

"I really liked Art, who owns the dealership, and he needs a guy around the place who knows how to work on old Harleys." He continues," I think this may be the Harley dealership I can work at for a long time."

EASTBOUND

The insistent ringing of the phone jolts us from our sleep at two in the morning on New Year's Day. I fumble in the dark for my cell phone on the table by me. Light blinds me as Dwayne turns on the lamp.

"Hello," I mumble.

"Mom, oh, Mom," Stephanie sobs in my ear.

I suddenly sit up and swing my legs off the bed. "Where are you? What's happend?"

"I'm okay. I'm just so scared and all alone. I want to come home. Why did I move to Washington, DC?" The sound of her crying fills my ear as she weeps thousands of miles away from me in California. She sobs about being on her own in a big new city and divorced. She has spent Christmas by herself for the first time in her life.

She surprised us with a new job in DC after Thanksgiving, saying it was a chance to get away from Austin, where John still lived. Dwayne and I had flown to Austin and loaded her belongings on a U-Haul. Then we'd driven to Arlington, Virginia, where she'd found an apartment. We'd flown home the next day.

Now I sway back and forth with the phone at my ear as if I were rocking her as a baby again. "I'm here, sweetie, I'm here."

Dwayne sits up in the bed behind me. He leans over my shoulder. "Is she okay?"

"Yes," I whisper to him. In my ear, Stephanie tells me a story of a broken New Year's Eve date and no friends like in Austin. I lean toward him and murmur quietly, "She's homesick. For us."

He quickly goes to the closet and starts to dress. "I'll pack us some clothes. I don't know if we can get a flight this late, but we can go to the airport right now. I got some money from that last car I sold to pay for some tickets."

He lifts the suitcase off the closet shelf. He lays it on the bed by me. He begins to fold shirts into it. He opens a dresser drawer and pulls out socks and underwear and tosses them into the suitcase.

I shake my head no at him, closing the suitcase on the bed by me. He sighs loudly in frustration and slides his feet into his black corduroy house shoes. He shuffles softly down the hall to the kitchen, and I hear him making coffee.

Stephanie talks and cries while I listen. She repeatedly apologizes for making us move her from Austin to DC after her divorce.

We talk about how hard it is to be divorced and alone. I tell her how lucky I was to have her when I launched out into the world alone. She reminds me that Dwayne saved us both. Finally, I hear her blow her nose. Her voice is calmer once the tears end. "Where's Dwayne?"

"He's smoking and drinking coffee. He's half-packed to come save you."

"Can I talk to him?"

I yell his name. He comes into the room with a cup in one hand. A cigarette burns in the other. Smoke curls though the air around his hand. He rarely smokes in the house, so I know how worried he is about her. I silently hand him the phone.

As I pour a cup of coffee in the kitchen, I can hear the murmur of his voice. The slow drawl of his voice fills the air. I lean back against the counter and close my eyes. Words float down the hall. "I love you, Steph. Do you want to come here? For a visit or to live?"

I curl up on the couch as they continue the conversation. Soon I hear him laugh—that lazy rumbling laugh that always warms me. I hear the snap of his lighter when he fires up another cigarette. I lie down on the smooth leather and try to relax. I close my eyes.

I feel the cushion by me dip with his weight as he lies down behind me. He curls around me. He lays his leg over me. I press myself against him. He kisses my cheek.

"Is she okay?"

"She's better now." He tells me that she knows she can come here to be with us. "She's like her mom. She's damn independent and won't give up."

"You're a good dad, old man." I roll over to face him. I kiss him.

"She's my kid, and I love her. Hell, I knew she was going to be a project when we got married. I just had to love her through the bad stuff."

We discard clothes all the way down the hall to the bedroom. We sleep skin to skin all night long.

The next morning Dwayne announces he told Stephanie we would be riding the Harleys to DC in July to visit her. "You're ready to ride from the Pacific to the Atlantic. We can check on our girl at the end of the trip."

We spend the next six months planning the trip. It will include a stop in Texas to visit his mother on her birthday. I mark the route on the atlas. We call Stephanie every Sunday to update her on our plans. I hang a map of the United States on the wall behind my desk in my office and mark our route in red

On a foggy Northern California morning in June, with a burst of noise, we roll onto the highway at dawn. I ride down the white line of an endless procession of roads. Dwayne shadows me on my right. We shift in unison. Across deserts and mountains our motors harmonize.

We develop a sign language all our own. Dwayne forms a triangle with his hands when he's ready for pie and coffee. A raised right hand is a bathroom break. By three each day we find a motel with a pool. We float in the cool water, letting our tired muscles relax. We fall asleep in each other's arms. The alarm rings at five in the morning. We ride into the sunrise, and we move relentlessly east toward Washington, DC.

In Louisiana a thunderstorm slams us on the interstate. Waves of water wash over us from the eighteen wheelers. Needles of rain fly over the windshield, stinging my face. I wipe the water from my clear riding glasses with one left finger while clutching the throttle with my right hand. With every blast of wind and water, the motorcycle shakes beneath me.

Through the dim light we see an exit sign. The neon-yellow Motel 8 sign appears like a mirage in the murky air. We peel off our soaked clothes in the room. He drapes them over the air conditioner to dry. We crawl naked into the bed. Shivering with cold, we hug each other tightly. I throw my leg over Dwayne's legs. I pull him toward me. We wrap ourselves in the sheets and blankets. Our mouths join in a kiss. We fall into a deep sleep.

We wake at dawn and load the motorcycles. Dwayne dries off the damp leather on the seats. I pull out the choke on both of them and push the starter button. The throaty sound of the engines warming in the morning air throbs in our ears. We check oil levels and clean mud off the windshields.

The front desk clerk steps outside to watch us. He joins Dwayne in a morning cigarette. He tells us it is his dream to ride a Harley across the country. He watches me load my tour pack and pull on gloves and a helmet. "That's a damn big Harley for a woman."

I turn to face both of them. "I just ride it. I don't carry it."

Dwayne throws away his cigarette with a snap and laughs out loud. "My wife is my road dog riding buddy!" The clerk waves an envious goodbye to us, and we swing out of the driveway.

We call Stephanie from Charleston to tell her we'll be at her apartment in two days. She can't wait to show us DC. That night we sit with a map on the table between us in a diner. We plan our path to her address over coffee and eggs. Dwayne tells me he has followed me across nine states, so he will just let me take the lead. He adds that if I disappear from sight, he won't be able to find his way home.

Trees and pastures become apartment complexes and free-ways as we roll northward into Virginia. We flow into the river of DC traffic when we reach the beltway. Dwayne rides closer to my right side as cars tightly pack around us. I cover the clutch level lightly with my left hand in order to be ready to shift down suddenly. Dwayne seamlessly trails me around each corner. I merge onto the highway after we cross the Potomac. The river glows golden in the setting sun.

We turn right onto Stephanie's street and see her red brick apartment building. She stands on the curb and waves wildly at us. She points to the parking lot behind the building. We cut the engines off and back into the parking space side by side.

Before we can get off, she hugs me and then Dwayne tightly. "I can't believe you made it!" She adds that she could hear our loud motors before she saw us.

Dwayne reminds her that we promised we'd visit, and we never break a promise to our daughters. Lifting our tired bodies from the seats, we both stretch our arms and legs. She helps us carry our two small duffel bags up to her apartment. We talk and tell travel stories late into the night. I look at the two of them in the circle of light at the kitchen table. Stephanie takes our hands across the table, and we sit linked like that.

She proudly shows us her new city over the next five days. We spend hours in the Smithsonian Air and Space Museum. Dwayne pulls us over to examine a Huey helicopter. "That's what I flew on in Vietnam," he tells us.

We sit on a wooden bench against the wall. Stephanie and I sit on each side of him. We listen to his story of hovering over lush green jungles lit by the yellow-and-red flames from gunfire and bombs exploding. It is the first time he has spoken of his war experiences with us. He avoids looking at us. He stares at the helicopter towering over us, and his chest rises and falls as he draws deep breaths.

His strong rounded hands with his sunburned fingers clutch his knees; the words spill out of him. "I was a sniper," he confesses. "A boy from Texas knows how to shoot. The army used that. I've spent years trying to forget that moment when my finger pulled a trigger and someone died."

We let silence fill us as he remembers, and we console him, listening in silence.

"I'm going to build a helicopter," he says. He wants to fly it himself. He wants to just enjoy the machine and the sensation of floating over the ground, to wipe out the bad memories.

Stephanie and I promise him, "We'll fly with you when you get it built."

The next day we put the Harleys on a truck to be shipped home, since it would take too long to ride home. School starts for me in a few days. We watch the truck take the exit ramp to the highway. I tell him, "We're going to take a summer ride ocean to ocean until we're in our nineties."

Dwayne says, "Hell yeah, we are."

We catch an early flight the next morning. We return to our work lives, with me getting ready for a new school year as an assistant principal and him back at the parts counter at Modesto

Harley. Now, sitting at my desk, staring out the window at the dusty, flat Central California fields, I feel again asphalt beneath my wheels. The scents of salty oceans and mountains with their smells of sand and pine fill my nose, not the odor of cow manure at the dairy farms surrounding me here. For me, the moment we return from our motorcycle trip, I'm looking forward to the next one.

GROUNDED

I return home at midnight from a football game at my high school and find Dwayne awake and waiting for me. I ease myself down on the edge of the bed. I close my eyes in exhaustion. My day began at six in the morning.

Dwayne punches the button on the remote, and the TV screen goes black. "Are you going with me tomorrow to Pismo?"

I swing myself into bed. "Yes, of course I am."

"On the Harley?"

"It's supposed to rain. I'll take your truck."

The conversation ends with my announcement. We know I haven't ridden for three months after the start of the school year. I got a new job as a principal at a large high school the spring after our DC trip. I leave the house early and often don't come home until late at night. I am too tired for our usual Sunday ride on our only day together.

I rest my hand on his in the middle of the bed. "I know my taking the high school principal's job has been tough, but I'll work on being home more." I have made the promise before. I never keep it.

Dwayne doesn't answer. He rolls over and turns his back to

me. I lie in the dark and listen to him pretend to be asleep. We have never had an argument, but this wall of silence seems worse.

The next morning, I drive Dwayne's truck on his employee motorcycle run to Pismo Beach. I follow the path of the long line of Harleys streaming down the highway in front of me, riding side by side. I watch Dwayne on his in the middle of the pack. His left hand hangs over his knee. He hunches over the gas tank in his usual crouched position. He always returns to flat track racer position on a motorcycle. I can see the large red number one on the back of his black leather jacket, the logo of Mitchell's Modesto Harley, where he works. He doesn't look back to see if I'm still behind them. I look at Dwayne's friend Steve riding slightly ahead of him on his left, my usual spot on motorcycle runs.

I lift my shoulders and roll them in an effort to ease the ache. I lean back in the seat and try to relax. I peer out at the dark clouds rolling across the gray sky. I see no sign of the promised rain. Patches of sun appear now and then. Ahead of me the motorcycles curve around the mountain road. I hear their rumbling motors though the thick glass of the windshield. It feels strange to hear a Harley motor from a distance instead of beneath me.

We drop over the hill into Pismo. The Pacific on my right gleams silver in the dim sun. The motorcycle riders and I drive through the line of palm trees into downtown. I park the truck on the curb near the motel where the rally will be held. I get out and slam the door behind me. I lean against the tailgate and watch each rider shut off his or her motor, then roll backward to park. With practiced skill, everyone lines up and gets off their Harley.

I spot Dwayne in the middle of one of the rows of motorcycles. I walk toward him and watch him laugh and talk with Steve and some of his other friends. I slip my arm around his waist and smile at everyone.

Everyone tells me hello and how sorry they are that I didn't join them. I say, "It felt strange to be watching you ride instead of riding with you."

Without speaking, Dwayne moves away from me. I follow him into the tent where the drinks and food are kept. He pulls up the lid of a cooler and hands me a beer. Its icy metal tingles in my hand. We push our way through the crowd and find a couple of lawn chairs. We sit down and watch the crowd for the rest of the afternoon. He doesn't talk to me much. His stories and jokes are shared with the parade of friends who join us now and then.

Early the next morning we wake to rain slapping against our room's window. I press against Dwayne in the morning chill. He turns and wraps his arms around me. I tuck my head under his chin. "I love you."

"I love you too." He strokes my hair and pushes a strand behind my ear. "I miss you."

"I haven't gone anywhere." My tears drip onto his T-shirt.

"Maybe not physically. I don't know where your heart is."

We embrace each other as the storm moves out into the ocean. The wind moans against the walls. I don't want to get out of the bed. Finally, we have to leave it and the room to go home.

We walk into the parking lot to find branches of trees scattered on the pavement. I pull my leather coat tighter against the damp fog. I wore my boots and jacket even though I wasn't riding. Now they keep me warm and dry in the mist.

Dwayne and I stand in the cold and look at his wet motorcycle. We look up at the sky and see more black clouds on the horizon.

"Let's put the Harley in the truck so you don't have to ride in the rain." I stick my cold hand in his jacket pocket.

He cups a cigarette in his hand as he lights it. "I need somewhere with a ramp so I can load it." He smokes silently and then flicks away the cigarette. He goes into the motel office.

When he returns, he tells me the owner told him about a nearby warehouse with a loading ramp. I follow his sputtering motorcycle in the ricocheting rain down the wet streets. I watch him ride up the sidewalk around the building until he reaches the loading dock.

I swing the truck around and put it in reverse. Dwayne guides me into position. I stop with a bump against the concrete. I jump out of the truck. He jerks down the tailgate. Together we guide the massive Harley onto the bed of the truck. Its tires sink under the weight. Dwayne ties it into place with the bungee cords he always carries.

He looks at me. I hand him the truck keys. "You drive."

We sit across the seat in the warm truck.

"I guess it was a good idea to bring the truck." I look at him in the dim light.

He doesn't answer but inserts the key, and the truck starts. We chatter about our jobs and our daughters. Stephanie has settled into DC and now has a large circle of friends. Jessica will graduate from college in the spring. Our talk skates over the thin ice of our tension.

The next Sunday I walk into the garage instead of collapsing on the sofa in front of the TV. Dwayne is changing the oil in my car. I sink down onto the chair in the corner. I haven't joined him in the garage since our move for my new job. Our Harleys sit side by side in the center of the concrete floor. My Street Glide's cobalt paint gleams in the fluorescent lights. I haven't ridden it enough to get it dirty.

Dwayne rolls out from under the car and sees me. He stands up. He wipes his hand on a towel. "You are wearing your jeans and boots. Are you riding?"

"How about a ride to the Starbucks? We always used to do that on Sundays."

He stands up and grabs my helmet off the garage wall, handing it to me. I pull my jacket out of my saddlebag and roll the Street Glide out of the garage. I sit on it and feel the vibration under me. Dwayne rolls up beside me. We smile at each other.

I flex my hand and accelerate. I lift my feet and swerve out of the driveway. In a few minutes, I fall back into the rhythms of riding and shifting. I hear his motor echo mine as we speed down the street. We sit at a table under an oak tree with our coffee. We ride home slowly. I close my eyes and feel the wind brushing my face.

The next Sunday we get up early for a ride to the beach. We sit on the patio and watch the sun rise over the flat fields behind our house. My phone rings on the table between us, and we stare at it.

I answer it. Dwayne slides back his chair, and I hear the snick of the sliding door closing behind him.

I find him slumped on the couch with the television tuned to a car show. "I have to go to my high school. The security alarm has gone off, and the police thinks there's been a burglary. I'll be back as soon as I can. We can still go for a short ride then."

He stands up and zips up his leather jacket. "I'm going to Steve's house, and we're going to work on his scooter. We'll probably ride somewhere and get a beer." We stare at each other for a minute. Then he leaves.

I listen to the sound of his motorcycle fading away down the road.

We stop planning Sunday rides because we know I will never be able to go. I lie awake at night and listen to the rise and fall of Dwayne's breathing. Since our move to California, I have been the one with the steady job, the one whose salary paid our bills. Dwayne's work at Harley shops made our Harley lifestyle possible. In the dark night, I know an impossible choice waits for me.

FAULT LINES

"**D**o you want me to just pack my shit and move back to Texas?" Dwayne leans over his knees and clenches and unclenches his fists.

We are sitting on a low rock wall at Pismo Beach. The rough surface digs into my thighs through the thick denim of my jeans. My toes curl into the sand. I peer into his face and squint my eyes in the bright sun. He stares back at me. His stony face betrays no emotion.

"I don't know what you're talking about." I lay my hand on his knee. Behind us, motorcycles roar as his coworkers arrive and leave the motel parking lot. He has chosen the annual Harley employees rally to confront me. It has been a long twelve months since last year's rally, when I drove his truck there.

He reminds me of how distant I've become in the last two years since I became a principal, the two years since our DC motorcycle trip. He doesn't look at me but stares at the waves pounding the beach as he describes how long it has been since we rode together on a long trip or made love or even laughed.

He seizes my hand between both of his hands. "You can just say you don't want to be married anymore, and I'll leave. I've been through two divorces. I can't stand for what we have to end like that. I'm too old for the screaming and fighting." He adds that I can just tell him I don't love him anymore, and he'll leave.

I slither down onto the sand and lean back against the rough wall. I stare at the ocean pounding the edge of the sand. A long moment of silence stretches tautly between us.

I reach up and take his hand and pull him down by me. Dwayne shifts closer to me. "Do you still love me?" I ask.

"I am always gonna love you. I don't know if that's true about you anymore." We sit in the shadows with the laughter and the motors roaring behind us.

I shake my head to stop him as he starts to talk again. I take a deep breath. I lean forward until our faces are inches apart. "I will always love you. That will never change."

I struggle to explain the twelve-hour work days as a high school principal. I describe how learning to be tough and unemotional at work has leaked into my life with him. "Excuses. All I have are excuses. Please don't leave me. I can't live without you." I finally choke out an apology for breaking my promise to put him first.

We lean against each other there in the sand. I beg him, "Please let me be your Mary again."

"You'll always be my Mary. My baby." He smooths away my tears. I swing my legs over his. We wrap our arms around each other and sit there without speaking. I lay my head against his chest, listening to his strong heartbeat pulsing against my ear. He rests his chin on the top of my head. He sings *I'm a Believer* and whispers, "I can't leave you."

Finally, we walk back into the crowd of loud and happy bikers. I lock my phone into my saddlebag. It stays there all weekend.

On Monday afternoon I face an assistant superintendent across my desk. She slaps her day planner down on my desk. She frowns. "We have to talk about what you can do to make the superintendent happy next year about your work here. You have to spend more time at weekend meetings and at the country club with the other principals. If you don't, you won't be back."

She runs her hand through her short dark hair and slips off her suit jacket. She perches on the edge of the chair in front of my desk.

I hold up one hand to interrupt the conversation. I tell her I will be leaving anyway at the end of the year. It won't matter if the superintendent likes me.

She shakes her head. "I know you and the new superintendent haven't gotten along, but if you work at it, we can fix it. Work some extra hours. Play golf with us."

Outside my window students yell and walk quickly to their next class. The bell rings. A tinny voice pours out of the speakers with the day's announcements. I tell her, "I am going to resign."

We argue for a few minutes. Finally, she tells me she'll give me a reference, but everyone will believe I was fired if I leave. I tell her I honestly don't care.

She bangs the door shut when she leaves. I punch in numbers on my cell phone. The ringing vibrates against my ear. "Hey, baby." I hear Dwayne's voice.

"I'm officially unemployed at the end of the school year. Let's go to Vegas this weekend to celebrate."

His laugh fills me. "Are we riding or driving?"

"We're riding."

We curve over the mountains late on Friday night. The neon lights of Las Vegas spread out below us. Our motors hum contently in harmony. The warm desert breeze flows over my face. I take a deep breath, and the sandy, arid air fills my lungs; I place my hand on my gas tank, letting the vibration shake my fingers, content to be back on my Harley again.

We shut off the motors when we reach our hotel. We back

the Harleys into the parking space. We sit there side by side for a few minutes.

He reaches across the space between us and lays his hand on mine on the handlebars. "I'm the happiest fucking man in the world right now."

I nod and smile in agreement, blinking back the tears. We pull our duffel bags out of the saddlebags and begin our reunion celebration together.

At midnight on Saturday we stroll down a casino hallway. I balance a margarita in one hand and my purse in the other. Suddenly Dwayne takes my elbow. The margarita sloshes onto my hand from the sudden stop.

He points to his left. The open doorway of the wedding chapel stands open. The glow of the lights spreads out across the carpet. "Will you marry me again?"

"Of course, but we'll never find anyone to do it tonight." I begin to plan how we can do it later.

He shakes his head. He tells me all we need is the two of us and a promise.

We walk hand in hand down the soft blue carpet. We stand on the small stage at the front. The smell of lilies fills the air. Points of light from the chandelier bounce off the mirrored walls.

We stand face-to-face. We vow to love each other. *Until death do us part. In sickness and in health.*

I swear I will always remember the miracle of our blind date and finding love at first sight. We kiss. I lay my forehead against his, and our breaths merge.

We go home the next day. I spend months looking for a new job as a principal of a smaller high school with less stress. He plans the opening of his long-delayed custom motorcycle and hot rod shop. We find both in a small town in Sonoma County.

The move to our new hometown happens without incident.

The superintendent's secretary helps us find a small house on the banks of the Russian River. I like the view. Dwayne likes the garage.

I sit with a glass of wine and my laptop on the deck one cool evening shortly after our move. Inside the garage he bangs happily on the roof of his '37 Ford truck, the first car he's rebuilding to sell. The phone rings. It vibrates across the table. I pick it up and answer.

"Mary, Mom is in the hospital in Temple," my brother-in-law Doug's voice comes across the distance. "It's bad. We need Dwayne to come here right away." I tell him he'll call him back as soon as I talk to him.

I go to the door of the garage and watch him for a few seconds. He grasps the welding torch in his right hand. His face is hidden by his helmet, and he squats on the hard cement floor with a gray car fender in front of him. I move into his range of sight. He turns off the welder and flips up his helmet.

"It's your mom." He stands up quickly. "She is in the hospital after passing out at home. You have to go to Texas tonight."

He packs while I call airlines to get a ticket. We drive the ninety miles to Oakland so he can catch a late-night flight to Austin. As I drive, he spills out stories of his childhood and of his mother.

I hug him at the curb and tell him I love him. I apologize for not going with him since school starts next week. He kisses me firmly and reminds me his mom is going to be fine, so there's no need for me to go. He runs into the terminal to be at the gate on time.

Every morning and every night we talk on the phone. I cradle the phone to my ear, listening to him tell me about his day spent sitting by her bed. She never wakes up. He talks to her anyway, and he sings old country songs to her.

I am walking through classrooms with my lead custodian when my secretary runs up to me. "Your husband's on the phone."

I run into my office and grab the receiver. I only hear sobs when I say hello. "Dwayne?"

"It's me, baby. She's gone. My mom is dead. I need you."

I tell my assistant principal he'll be opening school. I drive to Oakland and get on a plane. I see Dwayne when I drop down on the escalator in the Austin airport. We find each other in the middle of the crowd and hold each other for a long moment. He grabs my suitcase, and we drive to his small Texas hometown to bury his mother. The mother he called every Monday since he was sixteen. The mother who fixed him her special iced tea every time we visited her. The mother who played a mean game of Yahtzee with us. The mother who gave us a check for $10,000 when we moved to California.

ENDINGS

The day of his mother's funeral, I know Dwayne's not his usual healthy self. We sit in the small dim alcove off the main room of the funeral home. We breathe in the overpowering scent of lilies and roses. I look out over the crowd of people crammed into the wooden pews. Seldom-worn suit coats stretch tightly over the men's bulging arms. Dresses rustle in the fan's breeze. Tissues in sweaty hands wipe tears and sweaty foreheads.

Roberta was an important part of the community of Cameron, Texas, and today it appears most of the town is here to say goodbye. Every seat is filled. A row of people stand shoulder to shoulder around the edges of the room. The clear soprano of the singer fills the air with "How Great Thou Art."

Beside me, I feel Dwayne stiffen. His usually tanned face shines gray in the fluorescent lights. A small groan escapes his lips. He clutches his stomach with his right hand.

I lay my arm over his bony shoulders beneath the starched white shirt. "Are you okay?"

He shakes his head violently back and forth. Suddenly he lurches up. Jessica, on his right, looks up at him with confusion. Married last year, she has just told us she's pregnant with his first grandchild.

He quickly walks to the side door and leaves. I look at both Jessica and Stephanie and motion that I'll go and check on him.

As I walk down the hallway, I hear the organ music swell and the solemn voice of the minister begin talking. I hear the bathroom door slam. I hurry to it and put my ear against the hard wood. "Baby, what's going on?"

The silence is filled with the sound of his vomiting. I slowly open the door. He is kneeling on the floor. He rests his head on his arm over the toilet. I squat down by him and gently lay my hand on his head. "I've never seen you this sick."

He looks up at me with a tear-stained face. "I'm sorry I left the service in front of everyone."

I hug him. "Only your sister, Myrna, worries about funeral etiquette." A smile flits across his face. We sit on the hard tile floor for a moment.

He clutches my hand. "Mom is really gone. No more Monday calls. No more cards with newspaper clippings."

I touch his cheek with one finger and kiss him softly. Then I pull myself up and take his hand. He uses me to balance himself forward.

We walk back to the family room. We inch past his brother on the end and take our places on the front row. Myrna glares at us. I smile back at her. Stephanie and Jessica bookend Dwayne as he sits down. They each take one of his hands. I sit by Stephanie and watch the three of them as the funeral finishes with a long line of mourners parading past her pink-silk-lined coffin.

At the cemetery Dwayne and I get out of the limousine slowly and walk across the dried brown grass. The blast of August heat rises from the asphalt behind us in waves. In the distance we can see the narrow ribbon of Little River shining in the sunshine. We walk to Roberta's grave and stand stiffly by the bronze coffin covered in ivory and yellow roses. We lean against each other. Our bodies balance together as we close our eyes. I secretly watch him through half-opened eyelids. I wrap an arm around his waist and pull him closer. I lay a calm hand on his stomach. I can feel the muscles clench and relax beneath my fingertips.

The church hosts a lunch after the funeral. Somehow we make it through the sympathy and the photo taking. Usually Dwayne is the center of attention with his stories. Today he doesn't eat. He doesn't talk much. He often leaves the room. We go home early.

We leave his brother's house at dawn the next day. We fly home to California. School has opened while I was gone. I am busy the next few weeks with teachers and schedules and students and football. It takes weeks, but Dwayne finally agrees to see a doctor.

On the day of his doctor visit, I come home and find him napping in our darkened bedroom. I lower myself down by him and rest my hand on his forehead. My fingers register the moist heat of his skin. "What did the doctor say?"

He tells me the doctor said it was just the stress of the move and his mother's death. I curve around him. We lie awake but silent in the darkness.

At a home football game one week before Thanksgiving I see Dwayne in his black leather jacket coming in the back gate. He dangles his helmet in his right hand. I know he had a follow-up doctor's visit today. I watch him search the sidelines of the field. He knows that is where I usually stand. I wave from the edge of the crowd standing on the narrow strip of grass in front of the stands. He waves back.

We move toward each other, and I jostle people, pushing my way through the mass of fans. Several try to talk to me about their sons. I ignore them and keep my eyes on Dwayne's face, and he moves toward me with the same hurried pace. We soon stand face-to-face. The noise deafens us. The band plays. People scream. The loud speaker squawks the play-by-play.

He reaches over and pulls my head forward. He puts his mouth close to my ear. "The doctor thinks it's my gall bladder. They have to take it out. I had to take an MRI to confirm it, but they won't have the final results until tomorrow."

I close my eyes in relief. I feared something much worse.

The next morning Dwayne welds a strip of metal along the rusted edge of the 1937 Ford truck he is rebuilding. I sit in a lawn chair with a cup of coffee and the morning newspaper. Sunlight streaks the garage floor. Fields of bare grapevines blanket the fields and hills around us. The welder turns off with a hiss, and he flips up the visor of his welding helmet.

"Look, baby!" He points to the windshield and uses his hands to demonstrate how low the top is going to be after he chops it. I remind him he has to wait for the rest of the work until after his gall bladder surgery. I promise I'll help him over Christmas break.

His phone on the workbench rings and interrupts us. He grabs it and presses it against his ear. I return to reading the newspaper. I can hear the rhythm of his words as he paces around the garage, but I fail to pick up the individual words until I hear the change in his tone. I watch him across the tool-crowded space and see fear and panic move across his face. His hand whitens as he tightens his grip on the phone.

My heart races in my chest. I clench my eyes shut for a minute. As I stand up quickly, my newspaper floats to the floor. My foot knocks over my coffee. A pool of brown liquid spreads across the concrete. I take three steps toward him.

He senses my movement and cups his hand over the phone. "I have cancer."

A wave of dizziness washes over me. I step forward and clutch the edge of the truck door. The still-warm metal burns into my palm as I watch his mouth move. The words are lost in the hum in my ears.

I feel an urgent need to talk to my daughter, and I step out of the garage. I call Stephanie, trembling as I push the buttons on my cell phone. I hear the distant ringing a continent away. It is only when I hear her hello at the other end that salty tears fill my mouth, and I choke out the news.

While I am sitting on the front steps of our house talking to her, Dwayne eases the door shut behind him and sits down beside me. I say a hasty goodbye and promise to call later. We instinctively move so our bodies push against each other—shoulder to shoulder, thigh to thigh—the way we did on the first night we met at Chili's. Our words fragment into chunks of pain and confusion.

He stumbles over explaining where the tumor is located. As soon as he utters the word *pancreas*, our eyes meet. Ten years before, a phone call from a doctor told me my mother had cancer, a large mass in the pancreas. Three weeks later, she was dead.

Night falls across the mountains and the river. We sit unmoving until the chill of the cement beneath us cramps our muscles. We stand and stretch our aching backs.

We stagger through the shadowy house to our bedroom and fall upon the bed. We gently remove each other's clothes. We make love quietly. I cry myself to sleep and hear Dwayne's quiet weeping beside me.

After a month of surgeons' appointments and medical tests, I find myself spending a cool misty San Francisco morning in a hospital waiting room. Outside the window the Golden Gate Bridge rises orange against the gray fog. Red and green lights blink on and off on a plastic Christmas tree in the corner. My stomach clenches from the stench of poinsettias. A Styrofoam cup of lukewarm coffee with a skin of powdered creamer is clutched in my hand. I have been sitting here for four hours. My last view of Dwayne was the top of his mint-green gauze cap when he was wheeled through the stainless-steel surgery doors.

Now I rock back and forth slightly and try to convince myself it is going to be all right. We have been told there is a 50 percent chance they can remove the mass. I close my eyes and lean my head back against the wall.

"Mrs. Black," I hear someone say. I pop open my eyes and see a woman in baby-blue scrubs standing in the doorway. She's the one the surgeon said was his resident doctor. I stand up quickly. She motions me to follow her. We walk out the door, which swishes shut behind us. We face each other in the hallway.

She starts to introduce herself. I stop her. "Just tell me what happened. How is he?"

"We couldn't get the tumor." She explains the difficulties the surgical team faced. She describes the procedure they performed, rerouting his digestive system. I watch her lips move. Her words blend into each other. She stops and stares, then she takes a deep breath. "He made it through surgery, but we don't think he's a good candidate for chemotherapy. The survival rate for someone with this advanced a stage of pancreatic cancer is not high."

Her face blurs in my tears, and my voice cracks when I tell her to shut up. I choke on my angry words. A moan rises from within me. People walking down the hall glance at the pair of us and rush past. I turn and lean my forehead against the wall. I slap my hand repeatedly against it. *Thud. Thud.* I take a trembling breath, and the tears shudder to a stop.

Wiping my face on my sleeve, I tell her I just want to go be with my husband. She leads me up several elevators and through row after row of walls and swinging doors. She stops at the end of a long hallway. She reaches out with her right hand and swings open the door. She stands back so I can enter.

I see his white-wrapped form in the middle of the bed. Machines bleep and blink around him. His scarred mechanic's hands form a brown mound against the stiff bleached sheets. I drop into a chair by his bed. I place my hand on his arm. Minutes tick by.

Finally I hear him whisper, "Baby, are you here?"

I stand and lean over the bed. "I'm here." I move my hand to his shoulder. It's one of the few places without a tube or a needle in it.

"Did they get it?"

I swallow the stony lump in my throat. "No."

He opens his eyes. Nose to nose we look at each other. Our *I love you*s mingle in our breaths. Then he painfully shakes his head. I lean closer so I can hear him.

"Don't fucking let me die in California."

HOPE

I grip Dwayne's hand with my left hand as I fill out the forms in the oncologist's office with the other one. His knee jiggles up and down rhythmically against my thigh. Red vinyl chairs fall into a line around three of the room's sunny yellow walls. Someone sits in every chair in the cramped waiting room. Most of the women wear brightly colored scarves or knitted caps over their bald heads. Most of the men leave their hairless heads uncovered, with the exception of a few wearing baseball caps. Dwayne still has his hair, but he is wearing his Modesto Harley cap.

On my right a bulky man in a faded denim jacket writes on the same form as I do. He chews his bottom lip and pushes his black-rimmed glasses up his nose every few minutes. His wife leans against his shoulder. Her bony hands clench a fluffy pink shawl around her shoulders. She shivers and sways slightly in her chair.

I remember visiting this waiting room every morning for the entire two weeks of my Christmas break after trying to call for an appointment. I decided I would come in person. I would ask the receptionist each morning for an appointment for my husband to see the oncologist. She would check the calendar and tell me there wasn't anything available for several months. I knew we didn't have months to get Dwayne into chemotherapy.

Finally, after the usual apologetic denial of my request by the receptionist, a tall man in a white coat heard our exchange. He was Doctor Jensen, and after listening to my explanation for my repeated visits, he agreed to see Dwayne. The nurse whispered, "Pancreatic" across the small room. Dr. Jensen and I stared at each other in the silence echoing after the word.

Doctor Jensen leaned over the counter and placed a large tanned hand over mine. "Then I think she needs an appointment tomorrow."

Now I finish completing the form and turn it in. Dwayne and I press against each other as we wait. Finally, a thin woman with her blond hair tucked into a loose bun at the back of her head swings open the door. She calls Dwayne's name.

I stand with my hand out. He reaches up and grabs it. He wavers slightly, trying to balance himself. I cup my hand under his elbow to help him. His white face pales in the fluorescent lights. We follow the woman to a small room.

She smiles at us. "My name is Pat. I will be your primary nurse as you begin chemo." Her kind blue eyes twinkle at us.

We both smile back. I take a deep breath. The surgeon said he wasn't a candidate for chemo.

Pat assures us they have been successful with other patients with advanced pancreatic cancer. She guides Dwayne to the examining table. She helps him climb up. "I can tell he's a fighter."

The door swishes open. Dr. Jensen comes into the room with a flutter of his white coat. He carries a thick red file folder under one arm. He sits down in a green vinyl chair against the wall. He flips through the file while Pat weighs Dwayne and takes his blood pressure.

Dr. Jensen closes the file. Pat hands him a yellow legal pad.

He motions to a chair for me by the table. I sit down and shove it near Dwayne. I lay an elbow on his knee. We both sit and wait for the doctor to speak.

The doctor pushes his glasses to the top of his head. "I am going to write what we talk about on my paper. Then you guys can look at it later to remember what medical decisions we make. I find that a lot of people are so stressed by the cancer they forget what the doctor said."

We nod. We sit in silence as he describes the diagnosis for pancreatic cancer patients. He pauses. "Only two percent of the patients are alive in five years. I am not trying to scare you. I just want you to know the truth of the disease as you make your decision about treatment."

I curl my fingers over the edge of the chair, digging them into soft vinyl. I stare at a picture of a vineyard with rows of orderly vines behind the doctor until it blurs in my gaze. Beside me I feel Dwayne stiffen.

Dr. Jensen pushes up his glasses and pulls a piece of paper from the folder. He hands it to me. I stretch across the narrow space and take it. I look at the word *gemcitabine* in bold print in the first paragraph. I scan through the words, trying to understand what it is and how it will work. I start to hand the paper to Dwayne, since he is the one who will make the ultimate decision about treatment.

He pushes the paper back at me. "Baby, you keep it. I know I can trust you to understand what it means."

Dr. Jensen explains that gemcitabine, known as Gemzar, will be Dwayne's initial chemotherapy. He wants him to start in two days, and we nod numbly in agreement.

We all stand and shake hands. Dwayne and I walk out of the office. We climb down the stairs side by side without talking and find our car in the parking garage. I swing into the driver's seat.

Both hands grab the steering wheel, and my knuckles whiten with my tight grip. Dwayne settles himself in the passenger seat and leans his head against the backrest.

We turn and stare at each other. At the same moment we grab each other across the gear shift. Our hearts drum against each other. We moan in unison, and I watch the tears run down his cheeks.

Dwayne breaks our embrace first. He wipes my face with the sleeve of his fleece jacket. "That's the last time we're going to cry. You hear me? Now let's get busy kicking cancer's ass."

I nod numbly and promise to stay calm. "We'll celebrate with a Harley road trip when you're better." I start the car, and we drive home.

We can't sleep the night before his first treatment. We sit on our deck at dawn and watch the Russian River churn and splash over the rocks. I watch Dwayne's hand tremble when he sips his coffee. His jacket billows over his now sunken stomach.

The time comes to leave for the doctor's office, and we drive there in silence. Pat gets us from the waiting room. She takes us to what she calls the infusion room. Dwayne hands me his jacket. I fold it against my chest as he sits down in the recliner. Pat pulls a lever on the side. The footrest pops up. He leans back with his feet in his clunky engineer boots raised. Pat gently takes his arm with one hand and inserts a needle with the other. The needle is attached to a tube leading to a bag on an IV pole.

Pat begins to turn on the bag with the drugs for his first chemotherapy. Dwayne asks her to wait, and we both look at him.

With his unattached hand he pulls a photo out of his shirt pocket. It is a picture of him on his Harley. He hands it to Pat. "Put that up on the doctor's bulletin board I saw in his office. The one with his successful patients. This will remind him of what I want to get back to."

Over the next few weeks Dwayne goes weekly to Dr. Jensen's infusion room for his chemo. In the beginning I go with him. Eventually he gets stronger, and he decides he can drive himself. He assures me he is feeling much stronger. I start to argue but know he wants to be more independent.

On a warm April afternoon I come home on a chemo day to find him in the garage. I stand in the doorway and watch him working. He squats on the stained concrete beside the truck he's building. He welds a strip of metal below the open door. For the first time, I see his face in the bright sun from the window. His skin now shines brown in the glow rather than the pale white of the last few months. As I watch, he stands with ease and flips back his helmet visor.

He notices me standing there. "Hey, baby. Let's go out to eat tonight." He hasn't felt hungry for months now.

We meet in the middle of the garage and hug each other. "I'm glad to see you got your appetite back."

Dwayne laughs. "Hell, I had a Big Mac on the way home today."

I shake my head and laugh. Dwayne points to our Harleys in the corner. We haven't ridden since his diagnosis and surgery five months earlier. "Let's ride to dinner?"

I look at him in surprise. I worry about him riding again but keep quiet. I quickly change into jeans and boots. Then we ride side by side to the restaurant. After a few minutes my body remembers how to lean and to balance the heavy Harley. My left hand and foot remember clutching and stepping through the gears. Beside me I hear the echoing rumble of Dwayne's motorcycle. I smile for the first time in months.

That ride to dinner becomes a regular event over the next few weeks. We ride to the convenience store, where he buys his lottery ticket, and the owner shakes his hand to congratulate him on being back on the Harley. We ride to a casino in the next town and to the coast to watch the sun over the ocean.

Only the Thursday chemotherapy and the Friday nausea and dizziness remind us that this is not our normal life in the days before cancer.

Over dinner one night Dwayne tells me Dr. Jensen on his next visit will have results back from blood tests and a tumor marker test that will tell us how the Gemzar is working. We will both go to hear the news. I lie beside him in bed that night and listen to his breathing. In the dark room, a small glow of hope burns in me.

A few days later, we sit beside each other facing Dr. Jensen. He sits behind a neat desk with only a dark green desk pad on it. Handwritten notes of words and numbers haphazardly cover it. Now the doctor reads the notes in the familiar red folder containing Dwayne's medical history. He opens it and thumbs through the sections to find the test results. Over his left shoulder, I see the picture of Dwayne on his Harley—in the center, just as Pat promised.

Dwayne shifts in his chair. "Well, Doc, what's the news? I know I'm feeling a whole hell of a lot better. Still can't eat much." The words trickle to a stop. I take his hand and hold it in mine.

Dr. Jensen takes off his glasses and lays them on top of the folder. He smiles at us. "The tumor has shrunk, and the blood tests show an elevated level of healthy cells. I still can't make any promises for the future, but you've made a good start at beating the cancer." He tells us he'll write down the results in a more readable form for us.

Then he stands up and reaches across the desk. He sticks out his hand.

Dwayne jumps to his feet and shakes the doctor's hand. He blinks back tears as he drops Dr. Jensen's hand.

In a daze, we stagger out of the office and down the stairs to our car. I start to go to the driver's side, but Dwayne takes the keys from my hand. "I'm going to drive my wife home."

I open the passenger door and get into my seat. The golden hills and emerald green grape vines move past the windshield as we drive home. An old Willie Nelson song plays on the radio. I lay my head against the backrest, and I watch him driving for the first time since his surgery.

He turns to look at me for a minute. "I know where I want to go on our trip. Santa Cruz. That little hotel next to the beach and the tattoo shop where you and Jess got yours. We'll even ride the roller coaster on the boardwalk."

I sit up in my seat. "Are you sure you're up to that? That's over a hundred miles. We've just been doing short rides."

Dwayne takes my hand. "I want to spend time with my wife. My lover. My friend. Not my nurse. Okay?"

I lace my fingers through his. "I would love to be all of those things again."

We leave for Santa Cruz on a sunny Friday morning. Our Harleys rumble in the cool air. I zip up my black leather coat. I tamp down my helmet onto my head and snap the strap closed under my chin. I swing my right leg over the seat. I lean against my tour pack and take it off the kickstand. I balance myself in the gravel on the driveway.

Dwayne rolls his motorcycle up to stop beside me. He lifts his head to motion me to leave. He gives me a thumbs-up with his left hand. "Lead on, baby!"

I roll the throttle and leave in a hail of small rocks. Behind me I hear Dwayne follow me as we pull out of the driveway.

For the next two hours we ride down Highway 101 to San Jose before swinging over the mountains to Santa Cruz. We decide not to take the more scenic route down Highway 1. The curves and narrow road seem to be a more challenging route for our first long ride. We stop for coffee and pie at a restaurant in San Jose where we used to go when we lived near there. I watch Dwayne in my mirror as we ride south. He rides steadily on my right.

Finally, we pull into the parking lot of the motel in Santa Cruz. I turn off my Harley. I look at the colorful shops and cafés crowding the street leading to the wharf. Down a side street I can see the sign for the tattoo shop where I got my tattoo. The Ferris wheel rises from the boardwalk.

Time seems to shift beneath my wheels. It is not 2010. It is ten years earlier. We can ride over those purple mountains behind Santa Cruz and be home in Morgan Hill again. Dwayne will be healthy and strong. I will be a teacher again. We will be newly-weds beginning our lives together in a new place.

"Hey, baby! I'm ready to get my ass off this seat and get a cup of coffee." Dwayne slides off his motorcycle. He stretches and rubs his rear end.

I push myself off my seat and back to reality. We walk into the narrow, dim lobby. The large man behind the counter welcomes us. Within minutes we have a room key. We park in front of our room. We pull our bags out of the tour packs.

Dwayne opens the door. The king-sized bed dominates the small room. We throw our bags on the floor by it. From the blue walls to the pictures of shells and fish, the garish beach theme surrounds us.

We begin to laugh. Dwayne wraps his arm around my shoulder. "It ain't the Hilton, but we've stayed in worse rooms. Remember that one in Galveston? Even roaches wouldn't live there."

We lie side by side on the bed. I say, "Remember that time we rode through the Mojave in 105-degree weather? That room we found felt like heaven. I feel that way about this one. Being with you again in a motel."

We go to dinner at a seafood restaurant on the pier. On the

walk back to the motel, we stop and lean against the low wall separating the beach from the sidewalk. The orange-and-yellow sun hangs on the edge of the blue Pacific. A soft, warm wind ruffles my hair. Gulls squawk above our heads.

Dwayne pulls me in front of him. He rests his chin on top of my head. He wraps his arms around me. He holds me tightly, and I can feel his heart beating against my back. We stand quietly until the sun disappears behind the horizon.

In the dim light of twilight, Dwayne begins to talk. His breath tickles my ear just the way it did on that night we met when we two-stepped across the dance floor. "You have been an amazing wife. The love of my life. I promised I'd love you until the day I died." He stops, and I feel his chest rise with his deep breath. "Remember I kept that promise. It's just the day is going to come a lot sooner than I expected."

I start to turn around, but Dwayne pulls me closer, my back pressed against his chest. There in the dimming light of the coming night, he spins a web of memories of our life together. His drawl and gravelly laugh fill the air. I relax in his arms, and I look at the pulsing waves, listening to his voice telling the story of our life together.

Without speaking, we eventually turn and walk back to our room. We undress in the dark room. The neon light outside the window glows through the thin curtains. Sinking onto the bed, we make love with the surf crashing outside. We sleep curled together in the middle of the large bed.

Two days later we ride home, north on Highway 1 with the Pacific gleaming in the sun on our left. We swerve and curve together in harmony up the narrow road. Our motors echo off the rocks and steep hills. I rest my left hand on my vibrating gas tank. The motor breathes and rumbles beneath it. "Please let this moment last forever."

Dwayne roars up beside me. With only a few feet between us, we ride. Wheel by wheel. Motor by motor. I grab my throttle with my left hand and put out my right. Dwayne holds out his left. Our fingertips touch briefly in the warm rushing air. We break apart. I move forward to lead the way home.

JOINT DECISION

I watch as Dwayne struggles to shove his Harley backward. I sit on mine and wait for him. Our farewell party at his friend's house can be heard from the backyard. Bursts of laughter. Throbbing bass of the rock music. An indistinguishable shout of voices. But we've left early after Dwayne whispered to me that he felt nauseous.

The driveway in front of us curves steeply downhill. I plant my feet firmly on the concrete. I balance the weight of the motorcycle as I steadily push back to keep it from rolling down the slope. Now I look at Dwayne, trying to force his motorcycle up the slope.

Dwayne's friend Jeff also watches him take his motorcycle off the kickstand and try to back it up. Dwayne toes up the gear lever to neutral. Jeff and I watch nervously as the bike wobbles slightly. We can't see his face under the helmet and the large sunglasses. We can see him clench his teeth. His jaw muscles tighten and flex. He moves his feet to begin backing up. The bike doesn't move.

Jeff yells over the roar of our motors to ask if he needs help. Dwayne yells back no. Today is the first time I see him struggle with the routines of being a rider. We even rode to Santa Cruz a couple of months ago. However, the chemo has begun to affect him more physically. Now I worry whether his condition has gotten worse after the near miracle of his getting better.

His arms stiffen on the handlebars, and he heaves the bike backward one more time. His booted feet skid a few inches sideways. Suddenly the heavy Harley angles sharply to the left.

I watch as Dwayne's legs begin to quiver from the weight. I pop down my kickstand quickly. I jump off and run to the two of them. Jeff takes two giant strides and grabs the handlebars. He straddles the front wheel and keeps the bike up.

I quickly close the distance between us. I reach out with my boot and kick out the stand. The bike pitches onto it.

Dwayne rips off his helmet. He flings it across the pavement. It lands with a clang. He screams, "Fuck. Fuck."

I take a step toward him. He puts up his hand to stop me. "I don't want anyone's goddamn pity," he growls.

Jeff and I retreat to the grassy lawn. We watch him push himself off the seat. He sways slightly as he stands up. He turns to face the Harley and wraps one hand around the handlebars. Jeff and I watch in silence as his shoulders shake with the choked-back tears and anger.

Finally, he turns to face us. "I guess I'm going to need some help pushing it back."

Jeff swings his leg over the seat. He shoves it back to face the drop of the driveway. He puts it on the kickstand.

Dwayne gets on it and quickly pushes the start button. I hear the motor snarl and the clunk of the transmission when he stomps it into gear. I rush to mine and start it. I pull up by him. He doesn't look at me, and he glides quickly down the hill. He swerves left without stopping. I follow him.

We roll the bikes into the garage when we get home. He stays sitting on his. But I lean against the workbench and look at the

Harleys in the glare of the fluorescent lights. Their motors click and cool in the damp evening air. Frogs sing the blues on the banks of the Russian River. I close my eyes and listen to my heartbeat drum in my ears.

He gets off his Harley. "Go to bed, baby, I'll be there in a minute."

I stand by him. "Are you sure?"

He nods his head to tell me it's all right.

I go in the house and leave him there by the Harleys.

At breakfast Dwayne announces, "I'm selling my motorcycle."

I put down my fork with a clink and open my mouth to argue.

He reaches out and lays his hand on my arm. "It's just until we get settled and I get better again. I've had a lot of Harleys, and I will get another one." He pauses and swallows hard. "I know you won't be working in Austin. You'll be taking care of me. We're going to need the money."

I move my arm away from his hand. "I'm selling mine too, then."

Dwayne stands up with a jerk. His chair screeches back. "Goddamn it! You're not selling your motorcycle!"

"I won't ride without you. You are the reason I ride." I struggle with the words to explain how I feel about riding alone. I watch him through the blur of my tears.

His face tightens into a rigid mask and his hands clench into fists on the tabletop. He reaches out and grabs his mug of coffee, flinging it across the room. It crashes into the wall. The black liquid streaks down the ivory wall.

He slams his palm on the table. Dishes rattle. He tells me through gritted teeth that he won't let me do it. He stomps out of the house. His truck tires sling gravel against the wall of the house as he squeals out of the driveway.

I clean up the mess. Then I go to work as usual. I call his cell all day, but he doesn't answer. I drive home, unsure whether he'll be there. His truck sits in front of the garage. I crunch across the rocky driveway to the doorway.

He's polishing his motorcycle. The soft cotton rag rubs rhythmically across the creamy wax on the ebony gas tank. The Harley perches on the motorcycle lift as he kneels beside it. I see he has buffed the chrome engine to a gleam of stainless steel.

His hands stop moving. He looks at me. "I called Art today." He turns to face me. Art owns the Harley dealership he worked at in Modesto. "I'm taking the bike to him tomorrow. He's putting it on the floor to sell." I hear the dare in his voice.

"I'll put mine on the trailer with yours tomorrow." Finally, I walk away.

I eat dinner alone. He doesn't come in the house until midnight. He sleeps on the couch. I lie in our bed alone. I listen for footsteps in the hall. They never come.

At sunrise I hear the garage door grind open. I throw on jeans and a T-shirt. I strap on my boots and hurry outside. I watch from the front porch as he backs the truck up to the motorcycle trailer, and I hurry to pull and clamp it on the trailer hitch. Dwayne backs the trailer up to the edge of the garage door. He drops down the ramp with a metallic clatter. I lean against a tree and watch. The bark bites into my shoulder as I press into it.

He stands by the large shining Harley. He reaches out with both hands and seizes the handlebars. He pushes with his right hip until the bike stands upright. He slings back the kickstand, and he stands stiffly for a moment. The weight of the motorcycle balances against him.

Our eyes lock across the space between us. He breaks eye contact first. He rolls the Harley toward the ramp. I move behind him and put both hands on the soft leather seat. I push firmly as it moves up the ramp. Dwayne stops it with a bump against the truck cab. He puts down the kickstand and grabs a bungee cord.

I move to my Harley. I take it off the kickstand and copy Dwayne's movements with his. I grip the handlebars. Balance it against me. Push forward until the motion moves the motorcycle. Dwayne watches me silently. For the first time ever, he doesn't join me in moving it. I get to the ramp. I know I can't build the momentum to leverage the weight up into the truck. I watch Dwayne. He sits on the edge of the truck bed and looks at me defiantly. Minutes tick by.

Finally, he marches across the short space. He steps down onto the concrete floor with a thud. He covers my hands on the handlebars with his. Together we push mine to stand by his. We stretch and wrap the cords across them until they stand upright.

Dwayne bangs the tailgate shut. He swings open the truck door and slides onto the seat. I hear the motor start. I climb up beside him.

We don't talk during the two-hour drive. We watch the dry golden hills of California through the windshield. At the Harley shop his friends unload the motorcycles. We lean against the truck door side by side and watch them disappear into the glare of the fluorescent lights in the back garage door.

We get back home as the sun sets behind the mountains with an orange glow. The chill of the house greets us when we come in the front door. I begin to pull food out of the refrigerator. We haven't eaten all day.

Dwayne meets me in the middle of the kitchen floor. He grabs my hand. Silently we wrap our arms around each other. Dwayne rubs his unshaven cheek against mine—his unspoken sign of love for fourteen years. I kiss his ear back, as I always have.

We stand there, swaying slightly, as the darkness falls. I fix us sandwiches. We eat at the table outside. The shadows and the window light play across our faces as we talk about the move to Texas in a couple of weeks.

Later we slip into bed together. I lean back against him. We spoon in the middle of the bed. Naturally, he fits his body against mine, the warmth of him behind me. He throws his leg over mine. Now we leave a gap of a few inches near his stomach, knowing it throbs with pain.

"You gotta promise me one thing," he whispers into my hair.

I tell him I will promise him anything.

"I know I ain't leaving much in the way of life insurance, but you get yourself a kick-ass Harley out of it."

I wake in the night and lay my hand on his chest, feeling his breath come and go in his frail body. I lie awake, dreading the day I might not feel his breath under my fingers.

LONE STAR FAREWELL

2010–2011

❦

I thought that love would last forever:
I was wrong.

W. H. Auden

FULL CIRCLE

"I want to thank y'all for coming to our wedding." Jeremy holds his longneck Shiner beer high. "But I am especially glad tonight that my Uncle Dwayne is here." Jeremy is the son of one of Dwayne's oldest friends, the one who opened the first motorcycle shop in Bryan with him. He and Dwayne were also married to sisters.

The crowd around us cheers wildly. All of us stand on the dance floor of the local bar where the wedding reception is being held. The woody smell of BBQ drifts from outside. The wedding cake towers above a white tablecloth. The blue-and-silver icing celebrates the Dallas Cowboys. Everyone turns to look at us after Jeremy's toast.

Dwayne moves through the crowd toward the stage. All of his friends and family part to let him through. Beside me Janice whispers to me, "He was always scrawny, but tonight I can't believe how sick he looks." She pauses and softly pats my arm.

At the front of the room Dwayne hugs Jeremy. He clinks his bottle against his. "I just hope you'll be as happy as Mary and I have been." We all raise our bottles and drink with the two of them. Jeremy visited us a couple of times when we lived in

College Station as newlyweds, and sometimes he'd meet us for coffee on visits to his mom, Dwayne's former sister-in-law. We haven't seen him for years, and the invitation to his wedding was a surprise.

Janice turns to face me in the crowd. "You know when Dwayne and I got divorced, the only damn thing Jeremy and Bubba asked was that they not lose their Uncle Dwayne. My own sister's kids." She shakes her head. Her heavily sprayed platinum hair sways with the movement. She takes a deep drink from her beer. She remarks, "We were a wreck as a couple, but Dwayne was always a good dad and uncle."

I agree, "Yeah, he's a good dad. Stephanie needed one when we got married."

We stand and watch him shake hands and hug his Bryan friends. His starched Wranglers sag over his wasted hips. His black leather belt with a silver Harley bar and shield buckle cinches tightly around his waist. Wads of excess denim fold beneath it. His daily dress now consists of cargo pants and suspenders, but he couldn't bear for his friends to see him in "old man's clothes" tonight. He is surrounded now by a sea of black leather vests, starched pearl-snap shirts, and Stetsons.

Jessica joins her mom. Her one-year-old daughter, Elizabeth, in pink satin and petticoats, perches on her hip. She reaches out to me with chubby hands sticky with cake icing. We walk across the floor to meet Dwayne.

He wraps his arms around the two of us. "How's my girls?"

Elizabeth hides her head under my chin. I try to coax her to go to her grandpa. She refuses. Dwayne tells her, "You don't know me yet, but when you get a little older, you'll know I'm your Peepaw. I'm gonna take you and your mom for a ride in my hot rod."

Someone pushes the buttons on the jukebox. A Jim Reeves song. We look at each other across Elizabeth's curly hair. It is the song from our blind date. Dwayne turns to me. He reaches out and takes my hand. "Can I have this dance, ma'am?"

I turn and hand Elizabeth to Jessica, who has followed me. I slide into his arms. We press together. He rests one hand on my hip. He clasps my hand with the other. We hold our clutched hands between our chests. We glide across the dance floor in the Texas two-step. Step. Step. Glide. I wrap my arm around his waist, and he leans against me. One of his hands grips my shoulder, and the other lies on my arm on his waist. I balance the two of us, his feet stumbling across the floor.

"I'm dancing with my wife again," he whispers in my ear. His breath lifts my hair. He sings in my ear. A chill runs down my spine.

At the end of the song, we find our table in the corner. Dwayne drops down with a thud into the chair. His shallow breaths wheeze in and out of his lungs. Sweat covers his pale forehead.

I dip a napkin in a glass of water. I stroke his face with it. "You okay, sweetie?" He looks at me and nods weakly. We watch each other in the dim light of the candles.

The music begins again. Guitars and fiddles. People laugh and talk. Bottles clink. Pool cues click against balls in the back room. I clutch the damp napkin in my hand. Water drips onto my knee. We both open our mouths to speak. We stop before the words come out.

Dwayne's friends Roger and Jerry join us. Jerry tells Dwayne he just bought a shovelhead Harley. Roger says, "There ain't no better shovelhead mechanic than Dwayne."

Dwayne stands up to face them. He grabs the back of his chair. His fingers tighten around it as he pushes himself upright. He reaches down and picks up his abandoned beer, tilting it back for a long gulp.

I look up at them and listen to their loud laughter and talk about all of the times Dwayne fixed their bikes. How he used cigarette-rolling paper to measure the gap for the spark plugs.

Eventually, Jerry announces he has the shovelhead on a trailer behind his truck outside. He asks Dwayne to come look at it. They walk toward the door. Dwayne turns around and looks at me. He motions for me to follow them.

We walk out into the dark, damp night. A Texas November night. Stars blink across the vast blackness of the sky. A chilly wind bustles through the parking lot. Now a week before Thanksgiving, it has dropped into the forties. We move over to Jerry's truck. The shiny black paint of the truck shines in the glare of the lone streetlight. The shovelhead perches on the trailer stretching behind it. The motorcycle has been reformed into a chopper. The long front forks extend forward at a sharp angle. The handlebars flow straight up in ape hanger bars. Orange flames streak across the elongated neon-purple gas tank.

Dwayne whistles with admiration. "Damn. That's a good-looking scooter."

He moves forward. The three men step up on the trailer. They cluster around the motorcycle. The shadows of the branches of the live oak tree above them move across their faces as the wind lifts and shakes the leaves.

I stand by the truck bed. I lean against the cold metal, happy to see Dwayne immersed in motorcycles again. He gently strokes the smooth enamel of the paint. He touches the chrome heads of the engine. He folds his hand over the rubber handlebar grip.

A sentence floats over the space between us. Dwayne is agreeing to our coming to Jerry's house tomorrow. He tells them how much I miss riding. I am going to ride the chopper. I lean forward to catch the rest of the conversation. Dwayne is now telling the story of the time I rode through a sandstorm near Phoenix.

Roger and Jerry mutter curses of admiration for my toughness.

I stare at the shovelhead chopper in front of me. I walk over to the trailer. Dwayne's arm waves through the air to demonstrate the desert wind that day. I reach up and touch his elbow.

He turns and looks at me. He steps down on the gravel by me. He lowers his head and peers into my face. I see the other two men also watching me. I take a deep breath. I thank Jerry for the offer. I pause.

Dwayne's face tightens in the dim light. His hand reaches out and grips mine. I take a deep breath. "I guess I'll see you guys tomorrow morning."

Dwayne throws his arm across my shoulder. He hugs me close to him as we walk back into the bar. The neon light above the door flickers a welcome. I step through the door ahead of Dwayne. Dancers twirl across the dance floor. Glasses tinkle. The night of celebration has just begun. My first motorcycle ride in six months waits for me on the other side of midnight.

I drive us home, since he has become too weak to do it. Dwayne chatters all the way. Most sentences begin with "Remember when?" Then he urges me to remember a moment of our shared riding history. I nod and smile but don't say much. The ninety-minute drive home to Austin passes in a blur of reminiscences and passing headlights.

We perform our nightly ritual as we prepare to go to bed. Dwayne swallows pill after pill. I check the pump containing a small plastic bag of drugs around his waist. Then I slowly adjust its position until he's comfortable. I stack pillows against the headboard. I take both of his hands as he lowers himself against them. The pump whirs and clicks as it dumps the chemicals into his bloodstream.

I glide in beside him. I press my leg against his.

He says, "You were awfully quiet on the ride home, baby."

"I'm just tired."

"I can always tell when you're lying, you know. Your face shows everything."

I admit I'm nervous about riding the chopper. I remind him I rode a bagger, a big solid machine. The chopper is a rock star with its narrow tires and tall handlebars. "What if I drop the damn thing?"

Seconds tick by. Dwayne is silent. Finally, he reaches over and pulls me closer. "I just want to see you on a Harley again. I can close my eyes and pretend I'm right there with you." He pauses. "Even if I'm not."

My tears drip and puddle on the pillowcase under my head. "We better get some sleep, then. I am riding a chopper tomorrow."

The alarm at six wakes us up. I get out of bed. I silently dress in blue jeans. I dig in my drawer until I find a Harley T-shirt. I sit on the couch and buckle on my Harley boots. As I dress, I hear Dwayne get up and go into the garage. I join him. He has laid out my helmet, my fingerless riding gloves, and my leather jacket. I scoop them up.

We silently get in the car and drive back to Bryan and Jerry's house. I pull into the driveway. The chopper waits in the open doorway of the garage. Jerry waves at us as he comes outside. We shake hands. Dwayne and Jerry exchange some local gossip. I walk over to stand by the chopper.

Jerry joins me. "Are you ready to ride again?"

I nod silently. I reach down and pull out the choke. I tap down on the shifter and click it into neutral. I push the start button. The engine roars to life. I roll the throttle gently back and forth. The motor vibrates through the chilly morning air. Puffs of smoke swirl out of the exhaust.

I take a deep breath, and I swing my right leg over the narrow seat. I am relieved to find I can put my feet flat on the pavement. I reach up and grab the grips and pull in the clutch with my left hand. I pull the lever up to first gear with my foot. I ease out the clutch and accelerate with a lurch. The front wheel wobbles slightly as I move forward. I gently move the handlebars back and forth. I will need to push them hard to move the front wheel in a turn.

I take another deep breath. I lift my feet onto the pegs. I flick my right wrist on the throttle. The chopper sails down the driveway. I push firmly down on the left handlebar and up on the right handlebar. The bike and I swerve left out of the driveway.

I see Dwayne and Jerry standing in the front yard. Dwayne gives me a thumbs-up. I jerk up into second gear. I take off with a screech. The wind whips loose hair from my ponytail. The strands of hair sting against my ears. I lay my left hand over the clutch just in case I have to grab it to stop the motorcycle suddenly.

The chopper shudders beneath me. The rough pavement of the street bumps beneath my tires. A rock bounces off my knee, and the sting burns under my jeans. The muscles in my hands and arms ache from the effort of keeping the chopper straight in the road. I wiggle my shoulders to loosen them up. I check the speedometer. It reads fifty miles per hour. Shit. It feels much faster.

I spot a school parking lot ahead. I swing into it and stop with a heave, tapping it into neutral. I swing out the kickstand and click it off. I wait, knowing I can't go back to Jerry's yet, so I get off the bike. I want Dwayne to believe I took a long ride on the chopper. I sit on the ground in the shade of the lone tree and look at the bike. I wonder if I'll ever ride again.

After enough time has passed, I start the chopper and put it into gear. I ride back to Jerry's. I can see the two of them sitting in lawn chairs in the doorway of the garage. They jump up when they see me coming. Dwayne grins and waves to me.

I pull the chopper into the driveway. I turn it off and dismount. The men ask me how it rode. I tell them it was a bitch on the corners. We laugh together. Jerry goes into the house to get me something to drink.

Dwayne reaches for me. I lean against his bony chest, listening to his steady heartbeat. "I'm proud of you for riding a chopper. You're always going to be a Harley rider." He strokes my cheek. "Even when I'm gone."

THE LAST BIRTHDAY

The sound of hammers and drills coming from the garage wake me up on Dwayne's birthday. He is sixty-three years old today. Over a year of chemotherapy lies behind us. I trudge into the kitchen for a cup of coffee. A fresh pot waits for me. I close my eyes and pretend for a moment that time has reversed in the night. Clock hands have whirled backward. The sun has risen on a normal day where Dwayne makes coffee and goes to the garage to work on his latest car or motorcycle project. I will sit with him as he works. Then we'll ride our Harleys to the local diner for breakfast. A line of anniversaries and birthdays stretch out into the future.

I open my eyes to the present day. We have just returned home after two days in the hospital. A stronger mixture of chemicals has been pumped into his weakened body.

I pour the coffee into my mug and carry it into the garage. I open the door and lean against the doorframe, watching him work the way I always do. His welding helmet hides his eyes. His bandaged hand quivers as he tries to direct the flame onto the metal of the door. The former wreck of a truck now gleams in the fluorescent lights with its new stainless-steel bodywork.

Dwayne shuts off the welder with a snap. He flips back his helmet and looks at me. "Look, baby, I almost have the door where I need it. Do you think you could hammer it into place while I weld? I don't have enough oomph to do it."

I set down my coffee on the workbench. I take the hammer from his hand when he holds it out to me. He hands me a helmet, and I shove it on my head and pull down the visor. It will protect my eyes. It will also hide the tears streaking my face.

I bang and pound the hot metal as he heats it with the welder. Eventually, he can close and latch the door into the lowered roof of the hot rod truck.

We slide off our helmets as he shuts off the welder. I drink my now cold coffee. He points out all of the work he has gotten done this morning. There is a Harley switch on the dashboard for the starter. He laughs about how surprised everyone will be by that. He grabs my hand. "We're going to take the rat rod for a spin by our fifteenth anniversary in June."

I nod and ask him if he wants breakfast.

He shakes his head *no*. He hasn't eaten for several days. He lives on protein shakes now

He follows me when I step back into the house. He takes his medicine, and I eat toast and drink more coffee.

Then I hand him my birthday card. He opens it to find my gift. I bought him a helicopter ride over the city of Austin. He told Stephanie and me at the Air and Space Museum about his wanting to build a helicopter like the ones he rode during Vietnam. This is as close as I can get him to that dream.

He lays the printed page with the helicopter ride coupon on it on the table. He smooths it with one hand. I stare at the cuts and scratches on his hand from his last fall in the bathroom. The clock in the kitchen ticks loudly in the background. We sit without speaking.

Dwayne rubs his thumb rhythmically over the paper, smudging the ink onto his skin. "Thank you for remembering how much I wanted to fly in a helicopter again. I remember telling you and Steph that day in the Smithsonian." He takes my hand. "Do you think I am going to be able to do it?"

"I'll be right there with you."

He naps most of the day. His brother and our daughters call him to wish him a happy birthday. We drag lawn chairs out into the driveway in the middle of the afternoon. He raises his pale face to the weak March sun and lets it warm him. Across the arms of the chairs, I lay my hand on his. Neighbors leave their houses to talk to us. Some of them I don't even recognize, but Dwayne chats with them about their families and their jobs.

The sun sets in a blaze of red against a turquoise sky. We stack the chairs in the garage. Another day has slid away from me. He will go to bed early after the painkillers kick in.

I tuck the soft, worn blanket neatly behind the couch cushions when I transform it into a hospital bed. I fluff the pillow and lean it against one armrest. I clutch a quilt in one hand. I will tuck him in when he lies down. We don't talk about it, but he has moved out of our bedroom.

Dwayne leans on his walker by me. He softly sings along with the Louis Prima song blasting from the CD player. "Jump and Jive" fills the air. He taps one foot to the beat in his black corduroy house slipper. He reaches out one shuddering hand toward me.

I take his hand and sway with the music. We match our movements in a small dance without moving our feet. I lean over the walker and kiss his bony cheek. He smiles at me. Then I back away, and he rolls next to the couch. I grab both of his hands and brace myself. He lowers himself down on the soft makeshift bed with a groan.

I push the walker away with my foot while I snap the quilt

in the air. I fold it under and around his bony body. He wiggles under it until he is comfortable.

He settles into the pillow. "Can I have the heater too?" He can never get warm now.

I flip it on and move it closer to the couch. I plop down on the floor by him and lean against his arm.

He strokes my hair with a flow of words. "Hey, do you remember that time your scooter broke down in Vegas? We had just got to the hotel, and the damn thing quit in the parking lot." The story floats in the dim light of the living room.

I rub my cheek against the skin of his arm. I close my eyes and feel the blast of the Nevada sun. I feel the grease-slicked wrench in my hand as I remove my Harley's rear wheel.

Louis and Keeley Smith harmonize in the background, singing about strangers finding each other in the night.

LETTING GO

As I pull into the driveway two months after his birthday, Dwayne's sitting in a lawn chair in the middle of the garage. He has folded a thick navy blanket as a cushion over the hard metal frame. A small colorful quilt wraps around his shoulders. His walker with the red-and-yellow flame stickers waits by him. He clutches a small notebook in one hand and a pencil in the other. Stacks of tools surround him.

I step out of the car. I reach down and hug him tightly. "Are you working on something new to do to the hot rod?"

Dwayne moves stiffly away from me, one quivering hand holding his chest. He braces his feet against the concrete floor to push himself upright.

"Are you okay?"

"Yeah, I'm fine." He looks up at me. He reaches out his hand and grabs mine. "Don't argue with me." He clutches the arms of the chair with whitened knuckles.

I lean against the workbench, waiting for him to speak.

"Baby, I'm putting together an inventory of the garage. All of my tools and how much they're worth." He stops. He pushes back his thin, graying hair. "I don't want you to have do this." He pauses and adds, "After I'm gone."

"What the hell are you talking about?" My voice rises with anger. I clench my eyes shut and push back the tears.

Dwayne struggles to pull himself up from the chair. Without a word, I step forward and steady him as he rises. "I gotta do this for you. I don't want you to have to deal with selling them. It wouldn't be safe for you to have strange men coming into the garage and me not here." He snaps shut the notebook.

I interrupt him. I tell him it will be months before we even have to think about it. He lays one trembling finger against my lips.

I blink back tears. "I don't think I can deal with this now."

He moves my stiff body closer to him and pulls me against his chest. I can feel his ribs through his sweatshirt. In the middle of the cold garage, we stand together.

Finally, he breaks our hold. I follow him as he slowly walks back to the bedroom where we've put his hospital bed. He sinks down on the side of the bed. I sit down by him. The hard plastic mattress flattens beneath us. I lay my head on his shoulder. He leans sideways and lays his head on mine. We sit in silence. Above us, the ceiling fan clicks.

Eventually, I stand up. I swing his legs around and up on the bed. He leans back against the raised head of the bed. He closes his eyes. The bones in his face stand out in the glow of the lamp. I wait until I hear his breath deepen as he falls asleep. I stand and watch him for a moment. Then I shower and get ready for bed. I tuck my cell phone under the edge of my pillow. The alarm will go off in three hours. I will give him his second pain medication of the night.

The next morning the hospice nurse arrives early for our first visit. Dwayne sits propped on the couch. He clutches a cup of coffee in both hands. Barely healed cuts and scratches cover his hands and arms. He falls more now, and he bleeds easily.

The nurse strides briskly by me when I open the door. Her wiry gray hair swirls from under her colorful scarf. She wears a navy-blue shirt tucked into her jeans. She clutches a cracked brown leather briefcase in one hand. She stretches out the other one to Dwayne to shake his hand. "I'm Pam."

She straightens up and swivels toward me. She drops the briefcase on the floor. She takes my hand. She covers it with her other hand. Her short petite body stands straight at attention like a soldier during inspection. "You must be Dwayne's wife."

I nod stiffly and shift away from her steady gaze. She lays a hand on my arm to stop my movement. "You know he can be in hospice care for months. This doesn't mean it's the end of his fight."

I move away from her and sit on a chair across the room.

She sits in the chair by the couch and pops open her briefcase, pulling out a handful of papers. She and Dwayne lean forward to face each other. I perch on the edge of a small ottoman across the room. I sit tensely, leaning forward on my elbows, and watch the two of them talk. She nods energetically now and then.

Finally, Dwayne stands up. Pam hugs him. He shuffles over to his walker. We listen to his soft footsteps and the squeak of the wheels as he goes back to bed. She turns to me, and she picks up the briefcase. This time she pulls out a small plastic bag filled with bottles and syringes.

She marches across the room to stand in front of me. "It's your end-of-life kit." She holds it out to me. I get out of the chair and push her hand away. She drops it, still holding the bag.

My breath catches in my throat. My heart pounds. My vision blurs. I drop to the floor with a thump. Pam kneels by me. She gently pushes my head down on my knees. Her other hand rests firmly on my back. "Breathe. Slowly. Slowly. Breathe." Behind my tightly closed eyes lights dance.

In time, I stand up. She sticks out the plastic bag again without speaking this time. I reach out and grab it. I clasp it against my chest, feeling the hard edges of the bottles and boxes.

We move to sit down at the kitchen table. She explains how to use the liquid morphine and medicine in the bag. "You'll know he's in a more advanced stage when he's not aware of you or where he is. Then you'll need to use the liquid morphine."

She soon leaves. I stumble outside and sit at the patio table in the sunshine. I watch birds dip across a blue sky. For the first time, I notice the green grass and leafy trees of a day in May. I didn't realize spring had arrived.

Behind me, I hear the French door glide open. Dwayne steps outside without the walker. He walks slowly and deliberately to the table and slumps into a chair next to me.

"How're you doin', baby?"

"I am pissed off, but I don't know who I'm mad at." I stop for a deep breath. "And I'm scared as hell."

He reaches out and lays a hand on my shoulder.

"I just want our life back." I slap the palm of my hand against the glass tabletop. It rattles beneath the blow.

Dwayne reaches down and grabs a handful of small rocks from the flower bed by the patio. Wordlessly he hands one to me. I fling it at the wooden fence. It bounces off with a thump. He hands me another one. I heave it through the air. It shotguns into a bird house. The house tumbles to the ground.

Rhythmically we continue. Pass the rock. Hurl it through the air. Thuds of objects hit. Some rocks sail over the fence into the neighbor's yard. Curses fill the air along with the rocks. Soon my arm and my throat ache.

I drop my face onto my arm on the table; my body shakes with my sobs.

Dwayne clenches his hands into fists. "I fucking hate this too.

I don't want to leave you or Stephanie or Jessica." He hunches over the table. His thin shoulders tremble.

I raise my head and look at him. I lay my hand on his arm. He raises his head, and we stare into each other's eyes. I wipe away his tears with the sleeve of my sweater.

I pass him the last rock I still grip in my hand. He picks it up. We look at each other through our wet eyes. He pulls his arm back. He flinches with the pain. Then he slings it across the patio. It doesn't go far. It skids across the concrete and falls into the green grass.

We lace our fingers together. Time ticks by. Another day ends.

Two days later on a cloudy Saturday morning, Roger and his wife Emma arrive in a dusty black truck. He hooks up our trailer to the back of it. I help Dwayne to his lawn chair. I tuck his quilt around his legs. I stand behind him with my hands on his shoulders. We watch them load the tools into the back of the truck, and he pushes Dwayne's last hot rod truck onto the trailer. Dwayne talks about where he bought some of the tools and what he built with them, and he tells Roger to tell him when he sells the truck.

At one point Roger reaches up on a shelf and clicks off the radio. I tell him Dwayne always leaves it on, even when he's gone. "That radio has been playing for almost fifteen years now. The only time it was off was during moves. Then he'd turn it on as soon as we arrived."

Dwayne reaches up and takes my hand. "It's okay, baby. I won't be working in here anymore."

The four of us avoid looking at each other after his announcement. Finally, I turn and leave the garage. No one speaks when I open the door and turn my back on them. I hide in the bedroom for the next hour. I sit on the bed and stare out the window. I hear the thump and clang of the tools leaving the garage as they are loaded.

Eventually, Emma sticks her head through the open bedroom door. She tells me they're getting ready to leave. I follow her out to the garage. Dwayne now leans on the cleared workbench. Roger reaches across it and takes his hand. Dwayne tells him he loves him.

Roger chokes out, "I love you too, buddy." Their joined hands stretch across the scarred wood. Rogers breaks the hold first. He turns on his heel and walks silently to his truck.

Emma hugs me before she joins him. "You call us if you need anything."

Dwayne and I stand side by side and watch them drive away. The loaded truck and trailer bump over the potholes and coarse asphalt. I push the remote button and close the door. We go in the house. I perform our nightly ritual. Medicine. Helping him dress for bed. Watching until he falls asleep.

At midnight I creep quietly into the dark garage. I pull the door silently shut behind me. I flip on the light switch. The fluorescent lights flicker on. I stare at the emptied space. A stack of car magazines and mechanics' manuals leans in one corner. His radio still sits silently on an empty shelf.

One crumpled glove lies discarded on the floor. I reach down and pick it up. I press it against my cheek. I smell the gas and oil. The smell of Dwayne working. I kneel down and sit with a lurch on the cold concrete. I press my back against the wall. I rock back and forth. Minutes or hours pass. The alarm on the phone in my pocket beeps. Time for Dwayne's medicine. I turn it off.

I stand up with a creaking back. Rubbing the stained leather, I lay the glove on the shelf by the radio. Quiet surrounds me.

GNARLY GIRL

I'm on a Sunday drive with Dwayne when we see the gnarly tree for the first time. In the past, we'd always ride our Harleys on Sundays. Today we are meandering down a rutted gravel road near the small town in Texas where he grew up. He suddenly puts a hand on my shoulder. "Look at that tree, baby!"

He thrusts his hand across me and points at a large oak tree with his index finger. His gaunt face is animated with excitement. Seventeen months of chemotherapy have left him thin and bent, and his face has shrunken to reveal the skull beneath the skin. In this moment of discovery, I see the first sign of joy I've seen in him in several weeks.

I study the enormous twisted oak tree, standing majestically in the middle of the fence. The dark bark has split as it stretches around the bulges and knobs of the tree. Its branches point their clawed fingers toward the impossibly blue Texas sky.

"It's a tree from a fairy tale. A wizard's tree," Dwayne announces. He sighs and leans his head back against the back of the seat. He takes my hand. "That tree has a part in the history of this place. It has a story. It makes me proud to be a Texan."

I turn off the car. We stare at the tree.

As we sit there in the sunshine, we point out all of the images we see in the tree. Dwayne is sure he sees a bearded face, and I see the outline of a gnome. He moves to open the door to go touch the tree. I look involuntarily at the walker behind the seat.

His eyes fill with tears. We both know he will not be strong enough to roll himself over the rough gravel of the road to get to the tree. He softly releases the door handle.

In the weeks that follow our finding the tree, I forget about it. I'm busy with each day's schedule of medicine and doctors.

Dwayne has not forgotten the tree.

One Saturday his cousins Sandra, Gwen, and Janice visit us. We're eating lunch when Dwayne stops our storytelling and laughter to announce, "Mary and I saw the gnarliest tree on the river road in Cameron!"

The three women look at me. Gnarly is an unusual word for Dwayne—not a word in his Texas biker's vocabulary. He describes exactly where they could find the tree. At his request, I quickly find him a pencil and paper. He sketches the tree for them. The drawing has stopped with the cancer. Now the magical tree comes to life under his pencil. He illustrates every snaking branch and misshapen part of the tree. They promise to go by the tree on the way home and take pictures for us.

The email with pictures arrives later that night. He sits transfixed in front of the computer screen. He names it the Gnarly Tree. He tells me all four of us are now the Gnarly Girls. I lean across his thin shoulders and listen to his elaborate plan for the spring ritual with chimes and pinwheels at the Gnarly Tree we will perform soon. He wants me to play guitar music on a CD player.

Four weeks slip away in a flood of bad news. One evening the hospice nurse and I step out of the bedroom in our house where Dwayne lies in the hospital bed. I had to call her after giving him the liquid morphine. Forcing his lips apart, I dropped the medicine into his mouth. He doesn't recognize me when I talk to him.

Now, after talking about what's next for him, we walk back into the room. The nurse puts her hand on my shoulder. "He's not breathing."

"Neither am I," I whisper. I sit on the bed in the stream of light from the hall, with my hand on his stilled hand, until they come to take him away.

A numb month passes. One Saturday morning my daughter Stephanie and I wake early. She has come for a visit because we are taking Dwayne's ashes to the Gnarly Tree. I carefully place the bronze urn in the back seat. I wrap his Harley leather jacket around it. I want to make sure it remains upright in the seat.

We drive the eighty miles to the tree in silence. The tree appears before us as we turn a corner on the twisting, dusty road. Its dark green leaves rustle gently in the breeze. I stop the car in the grass and gravel at the edge of the road. We get out of the car and stand for a moment with our faces turned up to the sun. I reach into the back seat and pull out the urn. I hold it to my chest for a few minutes.

I walk and stand by the tree. Stephanie follows me. She stands by my right side and hugs me to her with one arm. "Thank you, Dwayne, for all you gave me. I can't imagine where my life would have gone without you." My choked words hang in the silence.

"Who I am as a person is because you loved me and made me your daughter," she says. Spontaneously, our words of gratitude and love flow out of us like water bubbling over rocks.

I take off the top of the urn. A large plastic bag filled with silver ashes and dark gray fragments fills the inside. I pull out the bag. I cup my hand under it and untie the top.

Stephanie turns on the Native American chants and prayers

he wanted for his spring ritual. I turn the bag over. The contents dust out onto the ground. The ashes puff into the wind and land gently in the grass. Our shirts are soon soaked with sorrow.

Then I hang a crystal in a branch. She puts a colorful pinwheel near the base of the tree. We do not speak.

As we drive away, the Gnarly Tree, with its lacy branches waving in the wind, disappears behind us.

ALONE IN AUSTIN

2011-2013

To have been loved so deeply,
even though the person who loved us is gone,
will give us some protection forever.

J. K. ROWLING

MIGHT AS WELL LIVE

When my car slides under the edge of the large truck, I relax. Double tires rush toward my windshield. *Screech.* The car swerves in a circle. *Bang.* The airbag slams into my chest. What feels like a giant hand pushes me violently back in the seat. Immediately the bag deflates. I fall forward. The car bangs into the median and stops moving with a lurch. I feel something dripping into my left eye. I lift a shaky hand to rub it, looking down at the red smear on my fingers.

I lean back against the headrest. "I get to die."

Seconds tick by. Silence surrounds me. My left knee stings with pain. My heart drums in my aching chest. My ragged breath burns in my throat, but I keep breathing.

The passenger door squeaks open. A large bearded man sticks his head into the car. "Ma'am, you need to get out of the car. The engine is on fire."

From the front of the car, a loud bang shakes the car. "That's the tires exploding from the heat." He urgently reaches in and drags me across the gear shift. My body protests the sudden movement.

"Stop," I yell. I settle myself into the passenger seat. He squats down by the car. He doesn't turn loose my elbow. His tanned face and worried eyes under his ragged baseball cap stare at me. He frowns and starts to speak.

I shake my head no. I mumble about finding my stuff.

"Ma'am, you're going to die if you don't get out of the car right now." As if to emphasize his words, the hood flies up, slamming against the broken windshield. Glass fragments shower down around me. Flames shoot out from the engine.

I would choose death for me. I can't choose it for him.

Allowing myself to move forward, I swing my legs out the door, and he puts his arm around my shoulders. He pulls me out of the seat. While I recognize this as the first time a man has held me in a long time, I take a faltering step forward. My legs collapse like Jell-O under me, and I fall onto my knees. The asphalt digs into my bloody knees.

He leans down and gently lifts me up. "We're both going to get the hell out of here now. Do you hear me?" I weakly nod in agreement.

He marches me away from the car. The force of his movement drags me along with him. I can feel his hands digging into my shattered ribs. The car explodes behind us. The heat blows across our backs. We stumble faster down the hot pavement. We stop by a semitruck that he says is his. He sits me down with a thud on the footboard.

Sirens blare and come closer. I lean forward and look at the blazing remains of my car. The ambulance and police car arrive with flashing lights and an avalanche of sound. Doors fly open. Men in uniforms surround me.

A police officer looks at me. "Who was in the car?"

I raise my quivering hand. "Me."

"You walked out of it?" He leans over and peers at me, assessing my injuries.

I point at the silent trucker. He just nods and pulls off his cap, rubbing his sweat-soaked hair.

The paramedics push the stretcher up to me. One of the paramedics clasps a stiff brace around my neck. Within seconds I find myself lying on the hard plastic of the gurney. Straps cinch tightly across my chest and ankles. I watch the pale blue sky above me move as they roll me down the highway.

Inside the ambulance a young man in a starched pale green shirt climbs in. His heavily muscled arms bulge from beneath his tight sleeves. In a flurry of movement, he takes my blood pressure, bandages my head, and cuts off my shirt and pants. He wraps me in a heated blanket. He lays a gentle hand on my arm. "Who do you want me to call?"

"No one." I flinch as he pumps up the contraption to take my blood pressure. "My husband died six months ago. There is no one to call."

The ambulance rocks beneath us as it speeds to the emergency room. The EMT and the driver lift the gurney out as soon as we arrive. They roll me through the automatic doors, which slap shut behind us.

Doctors and nurses lift me onto a starched white-sheeted hospital bed. Thermometers pop into and out of my mouth. Blood pressure cuffs pump and release with a hiss. Soft wet gauze washes away dried blood. My arms fall into a backless gown.

Finally, I am scrubbed, examined, and tucked tightly into the bed. One of the doctors perches on a chair by the bed. He reaches over the rail and shakes my limp hand. He introduces himself as Dr. Sullivan. "You know how lucky you are?"

"Am I?" He raises his eyebrows at my answer. He explains that it was a miracle I survived the crash and the truck driver arrived to get me out. I nod in agreement, since I know that's what he expects.

Silence fills the small room. The hushed sound of people and equipment moving up and down the hall can be heard outside the door. Somewhere a baby's loud cry rises and falls.

"I need a phone," I suddenly tell Dr. Sullivan. He hands me his iPhone without question, and he leaves the room to give me some privacy. After several frustrating minutes, I finally have the number for Sandra, my husband Dwayne's cousin. I tell her where I am and what happened. I ask her to call my work and tell her who to ask for.

Then I call my daughter. Dr. Sullivan returns and interrupts our tearful conversation to tell me he's sending me downstairs for an MRI and tests to determine if there have been any internal injuries. He cups my elbow with his hand as I sit up and swing my legs over the side of the bed. I shakily stand for the first time in hours. The room tilts around me. I feel a wheelchair bump against the back of my knees. I flop into it. I am rolled into the bowels of the hospital basement.

Strangers lift me onto a flat surface sticking like a tongue out of the massive stainless-steel mouth of a machine. A soft voice tells me to close my eyes if I don't like closed spaces. Of course, I open my eyes. Only cold steel and darkness surround me. I tightly close my eyes and imagine an Arizona road at sunset. My Harley rumbles beneath me. Dwayne rides on my right.

When I return to my room later, I find my friend Gina there. She sits in a chair by my bed and talks to me while my cuts are stitched. Twenty-eight in the left knee. Seventeen in the left hand.

Dr. Sullivan arrives with a clipboard in hand. His green scrub coat flutters behind him. He frowns at me as he stands by my bed.

I look up at him. "I'm not going home, am I?"

He shakes his head no, taking a deep breath. "Your tests were negative for any internal damage from the wreck." He moves to the bed and pulls my gown away from my shoulder. He points to the deep purple bruises covering my chest and tells me they're from the seat belt. They will heal in a few weeks.

He tucks my gown back on my shoulder. "We found a large mass in your right ovary. Do you know what that may mean?"

I nod. I understand all too well what a cancer diagnosis means. I choke out that I have lost two people I loved to cancer.

Dr. Sullivan stands quietly for a few minutes. He finally tells me there will be extensive tests in the next few hours. He leaves, and the door hisses shut behind him.

I tell Gina to go home. I need to be by myself to face the tests and the outcome. I watch her leave the room and lie back against my flat pillow.

One agonizingly painful test after another follow each other through the night. In a dark room at midnight, I am lying on a cold metal table with my head down and my legs up at a ninety-degree angle. Someone thrusts a slick icy object into me. I cry out in pain. A disembodied voice tells me to be brave.

The ordeal ends at three in the morning. Getting out of bed after the last nurse leaves the room, I push the lone chair to face the window. I sit on the smooth chilly vinyl, wrapped in a blanket. The shadowy trees outside wave back and forth in a gentle wind. I press my hand against the cool glass. The darkness outside outlines my pale fingers. The lamp over the bed glows in the background. I have spent six months longing for death. I wake each morning to the disappointment of a beating heart.

I whisper to myself, "Our love story won't end with us dying together."

A flood of images of surgery and chemo fills me. Dwayne's pale face when the hospice nurse told me he wasn't breathing. Rosary bead memories of our life together click through my mind. The joy and the love of our marriage buried under the sorrow.

Sandra is with me when Dr. Sullivan arrives early the next

morning. He clutches a stack of papers in one hand. He grabs the clipboard from the foot of the bed, and he clicks it open with a snap. He shoves his papers in it.

Moving to stand by my bed, he flips through the pages and tells me the results of the tests. I have a fibroid tumor. Not cancer.

He sticks his hand out toward me. I hesitate and then raise my hand from the bed. He takes my limp hand in his and holds it gently. "You're mighty lucky, Mrs. Black. You've cheated death twice in twenty-four hours."

I whisper softly to myself, "Death cheated me twice in one day." Sandra and Dr. Sullivan watch me, and they lean forward to listen to my soft words.

I shake my head back and forth and tell them the lie that it's not important. I am dismissed and sent home to heal.

Two days later Gina takes me for a follow-up appointment with the doctor. The check-up only lasts a short time, and then she drives me back to my house. As she helps me out of the car, she looks at Dwayne's truck still sitting in the driveway six months after his death. "Are you going to drive the truck now?"

I lean against the car door and stare at the white Chevy truck. It hasn't been moved since Dwayne parked it on a Saturday night after buying a lottery ticket. His last one. He died three days later. "I honestly don't know if I can drive it."

Gina walks with me to the front door. "Have you ever bought a car by yourself?"

I swing open the door and shake my head. "No. Dwayne was the car expert." I tell her I am on my own now.

The next week is Thanksgiving, and I limp on a plane to fly to Washington, DC. I share turkey and pie with Stephanie and her boyfriend, Ben. When my plane lands in Austin, I take a shuttle home from the airport.

Then, early Monday morning, I push the button by the back

door. The garage door rolls up with a squawk. The truck waits for me in the driveway. I clutch its keys in my right hand. I found them where he left them on top of the refrigerator, his daily habit when he got home.

I click the remote. The lights blink on, and the locks click open. I push my purse strap up on my shoulder. I take a deep breath. I walk slowly to the driver's door. I wrap my fingers around the handle. I pull it open.

The dusty air inside the truck cab rushes out. His Modesto Harley hat sits crumpled on the front seat. Beside it, the lottery ticket in its plastic envelope curls from the heat. On the floor, several discarded empty bottles of Starbucks Frappuccino lie scattered—the only thing he liked to drink at the end.

I slam the door shut. There in the driveway with cars passing by, I press my forehead against the chilly glass in the weak November sunshine.

"I cannot fucking do this." I focus on breathing. In and out. In and out.

After a few minutes, I open the door again. I quickly step up on the running board and slide onto the cold vinyl seat. I throw the cap and the lottery ticket into the back seat. I stick the key in the ignition and turn it. The engine roars to life.

Music blares out of the speakers. Louis Prima and Keely Smith. "Jump, Jive, an' Wail." An image of the two of us dancing across the kitchen floor to Louis Prima races across my memory. I hit the eject button. The CD pops out. I throw it over my shoulder to the back seat to join the other stuff.

I reverse out of the driveway with a lurch. The empty bottles rattle against each other as they roll around on the floor. I drive to work and sit in the garage with my head on the steering wheel, watching the minutes drop by on the clock. Eventually, I wipe my eyes and blow my nose and go through the daily routines of work.

On Saturday morning I drive to the nearest Chevy dealer. A smiling salesman rushes out of the building. "Can I help you, ma'am?"

"I need a car." I hand him the truck keys and the insurance check I got in the mail. "Whatever I can get with the truck as a trade-in and the check, I will buy."

He looks down at the keys and the check fluttering in the breeze. "I have a Malibu I think you'll like."

We look at each other without speaking. I turn to scan the cars on the lot. "Let's go look at it."

I drive home an hour later in my new car. In my rearview mirror, I watch them drive the truck into the used-car garage to be prepped for selling. In a brown paper bag by me on the passenger seat are all of his belongings from the truck. I reach in the bag and pull out the Prima CD. I push it into the stereo. Louis sings me home.

THE RING

I don't notice it, but evidently I have been sighing a lot the last few months since my wreck in November. Tonight I went to my first grief group meeting.

"You actually forget to breathe," the hospice counselor says. She tells us that excessive sighing is a symptom of grief.

All of us in the group sit in silence as we consider whether we are sighing more. I stop and feel the breath flowing in and out of my nose. I glance around at the others sitting around the table with me: seven women and two men. The youngest is twenty-seven and the oldest is sixty-eight. Cancer has crippled all of us.

None of us have removed our wedding rings yet. They glint in the fluorescent lights. To the rest of the world, they proclaim we are still married, but in this room we know the union has been broken forever. We are now single and alone.

The counselor announces that we will all share our story, since this is our first meeting. My stomach clenches in anticipation of saying Dwayne's name and using the word *dead* to describe him. I sit up straight in the hard chair. I focus on one of the inspirational posters on the wall. Luminous sunlight pierces dark thunder-clouds in the picture. *Light always breaks through the darkness.*

What a lie, I think. I believe darkness usually wins the fight.

I listen to each tale of sorrow and loss. I tense when the woman sitting by me finishes her story. I take a deep breath and begin. I roll the tissue in my hand into a tight ball and grip it while I describe what hospice calls "my cancer experience." I finish as quickly as possible.

Finally, the evening ends with a moment of silence for our lost loved ones. I rush out of the room and drive quickly home. When the garage door rolls up, I am again stunned by the emptiness. No tools on the wall. An empty workbench. No half-built car or motorcycle waiting to be created.

Crawling into bed without removing my clothes, I clutch the pillow on his empty side of the bed to my chest. I stare at the soft glimmer of my neighbor's yard light outside my window until I fall asleep.

The next day at work I tell my friend Gina about the counselor's describing the excessive sighing from grief. All that day I feel her step into my cubicle and lay a gentle hand on my shoulder when I sit frozen in front of my computer screen. Sighing. Not breathing.

I take a deep breath. I nod. She smiles and walks away.

Spring turns into summer. Each Monday I return to Hospice Austin. The rest of the week I go home right after work. I walk quietly down the hallway past the closed door of the room where Dwayne died. I never open it. I go directly to bed and wait out the night.

The hospice grief group ends, and I decide not to sign up for the next series of meetings. I can't imagine sitting through another introductory meeting and talking about the dark void inside of me.

On some nights after work, I begin to stop for dinner at restaurants on the way home. I sit alone at the counter, where it is easier to eat alone. Everyone knows you are by yourself when you sit on one side of a booth with no one on the other side. I watch the crowd of couples enter and leave the booths and tables.

One night an older man and woman lean toward each other with the light from the candles on each table flickering across their faces. He leans over the plates to look at her as she talks. I check to see whether they wear wedding rings. They do. I look down at the ring still on my left hand and envy them their future.

On the second anniversary of Dwayne's death, I stop outside the closed bedroom door, one hand on the doorknob. The room where he died. Cautiously I open it. The musty smell of an unused room drifts past me. I drop down on the bed. I reach over and pull out a drawer of the nightstand. I stare at his dead cell phone. His reading glasses sit on top of a hot rod magazine. A small box is jammed into the back of the drawer.

I open it. The carved silver Harley ring he wore for over forty years lies inside, the one I saw on our blind date. In those last months, he got so thin the ring kept falling off his finger, so we put it away. I close the box. I clutch it in my hand for a moment and then put it back in the drawer.

I curl up on the bed, and the room darkens as the sun goes down. Finally, I close the door behind me and go to my bed.

Now after that first opening of the door, I sit in the room every day after work for several weeks. I know I am surrounded by all of his possessions, since he always used the guest room for his clothes. During his illness, we put his hospital bed in here, inside these walls, where he stopped breathing.

One day as I sit there in the silent room, I call Dwayne's cousin Sandra, now my cousin. "I'm ready to clean out Dwayne's stuff. Can you help me Sunday?"

Sandra arrives early on that day. She hugs me tightly when she steps through the door. We don't talk. Over the next hour we empty the drawers in the chest. We pull clothes off hangers in the closet. Some we put in a carved wooden trunk for me to keep, and some go into the Goodwill bag.

We throw out dated magazines and wadded auto parts receipts. We discover scattered stacks of small pieces of paper filled with notes, drawings, and phone numbers. Some of these also go in the chest, while others go in the trash.

Our packing develops a mechanical rhythm. Sandra hands things to me, and I decide the fate of each article. I force myself to make the decision as quickly as possible. When we come to the box with the ring, I pull it out and push it slowly onto my thumb. Its weight hangs loosely against my knuckle.

Finally, we stand in the middle of the pile of boxes and bags. I allow myself a deep sigh, and I breathe. My chest aches with its rise and fall.

As we load the boxes into her car for her to take to Goodwill, we stop and look at the Harley cabinet in the corner of the living room. Dwayne spent weeks refinishing it. He painstakingly painted a Harley bar and shield emblem on the front. My first Harley boot buckles were turned into door handles. Inside sits a lifetime of Harley memorabilia.

I turn to Sandra. "I know where this belongs. Wild Bill's motorcycle shop in Bryan." Wild Bill from the Bryan Harley dealer, where Dwayne worked when we were first married. The one who shook my hand and called me Dwayne's Mary all those years ago when I visited the first Harley shop where Dwayne worked after our marriage.

The next day I call and ask him if he could find a spot in the shop for the cabinet.

He immediately says, "You know how much I loved Dwayne. I'll put it where everyone sees it as soon as they walk in."

The next Saturday a neighbor helps me load the cabinet and

boxes into the back of a rented truck. I drive the ninety miles to Dwayne's hometown and the town where we began our married life. I find the motorcycle shop and park in front of the garage doors.

Bill arrives with a roar on his Harley a few minutes later. He rolls up the large door. We unload the boxes. We carry the cabinet to a wall in the showroom, and Bill describes the way he wants to make it a showcase of Dwayne's life in motorcycles. I nod and rub one finger on the glossy surface of the wood.

On the way home, I drive to our first house on Dowling Road. I park the truck on the edge of the road. I look at the small green house under the large live oak tree. The garage where we built our shovelhead Harley. The front porch where we drank our morning coffee.

I reach into my purse and pull out the Harley ring from an inside pocket. I slide my wedding ring off my finger. I ease both of them onto a silver chain and fasten it around my neck. The world will now know I am an unmarried woman. I drive away and leave Bryan behind.

I draw breath.

THE PROMISE

"You'll be on a Harley in no time," the girl kneeling at my feet tells me as she tightens and ties the last boot on my foot. She smiles up at me. Her deft tattooed hands snap the Velcro straps in place across the laced-up boot.

I stand up and wiggle my feet inside the stiff new boots. I dangle the flip flops I wore to the Harley shop in my right hand. Around me the chrome and paint on the new motorcycles reflect the fluorescent lights. "I never intended to ride one today," I tell the girl. I explain I was only looking.

"How's long has it been since you've been on one?" She stands up to face me.

"I sold mine four years ago." I take a deep breath and think about the reason I sold it.

Pete joins us. "Hey, are you ready to go?" He is my salesman and Harley friend for the day. I turn to look at him in his black Harley tee, black jeans, and boots. His crew cut shows only a fuzz of blond hair on his head. Tattoo flames curl out of his orange T-shirt and up his neck.

I nod to tell him I'm ready. I follow him out of the shop. We head to a large white tent in the corner of the parking lot. Line after line of used Harleys stand in regimented rows under the canvas. They are grouped by model. Sportsters, as the smallest, stretch out in the first row. Electra Glides, as the largest bikes, hulk in a line in the last row. We stop at the Sportster row.

"Ah, the girl bikes first." I sigh. Pete leans his head to one side while he considers my comment. I assure him it's fine. After this long, it may be what I need. I wonder what Dwayne would say.

I grab the handlebar of the first Sportster. I lift it off the kickstand and swing the handlebars straight. I hear my heart beating loudly in my ears. I settle into the seat. My legs quiver slightly when I feel the unfamiliar weight. Then I push the starter button. The motor vibrates through the seat and up my back. Quickly, I shift up and roll the throttle, lifting my feet up on the pegs. The motorcycle turns awkwardly as I guide it to the rear of the parking lot. My hand covers the clutch lever as I ease into the rhythm of riding. Shift. Accelerate. Lean and turn.

I make five circles around the building and the lot. On the first circle, Pete is standing in the empty spot under the tent. He sticks his thumb up when I go by him. I hold my left thumb up to let him know I'm okay. By the final circle, I see him sitting at the picnic table on the far side of the tent. He gets up and watches me while I stop the Sportster and push it back into its space.

I join him at the table. We perch on the edge of it, and our booted feet rest on the bench. Around us the explosive sound of motorcycle motors roar when Harleys race in and out of the parking lot. I close my eyes. The sun warms my face. I hear Pete's lighter click when he fires up a cigarette. I smell the smoke curling across my nose, and I remember the smell of Dwayne's Marlboros.

I slide off the picnic table and turn to tell Pete I'm leaving. Then I stop.

He stands up. He crushes the cigarette butt in the asphalt. "What's next?"

"I'm going to ride the black Road King there." I point to it.

"Yes, ma'am." He grins at me.

I stand by the Road King for a few minutes. Its black surface gleams in the sunshine. It's a mirror image of my first Harley. I deliberately slow my breathing when I push myself onto the seat. I can't slow my speeding heart. Trembling with nervousness, I repeat the ritual of starting a Harley. The motor comes to life beneath me.

Slowly I ease it past its neighbors in the row, each massive bike only inches away from my handlebars. I balance it while it mumbles and pulses in first gear. Then at the end of the row I simultaneously flick my right wrist and flex my left hand to grab the clutch. I step down on the shift lever. The Road King leaps forward. I sway in the seat. The King gently swings with me when I curve away from the other motorcycles. At the driveway entrance I stop the motorcycle with my feet on the pavement. The tent and Pete wait on my left. The street stretches to my right. The motor beneath me beats in a steady rhythm. Its heat warms the inside of my legs.

"Here we go, Dwayne." I turn right. The wind rushes past my face. I bobble my head with the unexpected weight of the helmet. My skin tingles with the forgotten pleasure of riding on two wheels with the wind pushing past my face.

With surprise, I hear the growl of another motor. It comes closer and closer. I look to my right. Pete has joined me on an orange-and-black Harley with tall ape hanger handlebars. Side by side we roll down the street. We weave in and out of a neighborhood. I don't see him. I only hear the sound of his engine. I am in a tunnel of time where it is Dwayne on my right.

Finally, we return to the Harley dealership. We park together at the front of the store. Pete gets off his bike, and he pulls off his helmet. "Damn, girl, you can ride!" He laughs and holds up his hand with the palm toward me, waiting for me to slap his palm with mine in a high five of celebration. He drops it when he sees I am still clutching the handlebars.

I sit on the now quiet Harley. The motor clicks and cools beneath me.

Pete moves to my side. He frowns as he lays his hand on my shoulder. Minutes tick by. Eventually, I wipe my sweaty hand across my face. I unfasten my helmet and swing one leg over the seat. I sit bent over my knees.

Pete kneels down by me. I tell him about my promise to buy a kick-ass Harley. I tell him about Dwayne and his love of Harleys—and me.

I stand up and say I won't be buying a Harley today. "Someday I'll be ready to buy that Harley. Not today."

I drive away from the Harley shop and the crowd of motorcycles. Pete stands in the middle of the parking lot and watches me leave, raising his hand in goodbye.

I wave back and go home to an empty garage. I lean against my car in the dim light. The dying sunlight streams across the cold gray concrete. The ghosts of our motorcycles seem to appear side by side there in the shadows.

I close my eyes, and in the bleak space I feel again the vibration of a V-twin motor breathing beneath me. I stretch out my arms and imagine flying through the wind on two wheels. Silence brings me back. No echoing motor on my right. The fearless Harley rider inside me still hasn't been resurrected. Not yet. She's still missing.

Then I turn on his radio, and the music echoes through the abandoned space. I walk away and leave a Harley-sized space in the garage and in my life.

ACKNOWLEDGMENTS

Like grief itself, writing often forces someone into isolation and solitary reflection, but getting my story of Dwayne and our love story and Harley life shared and published took a community of supporters. With heartfelt gratitude I thank all of you.

For Dwayne, you'll live again within these pages for all of my readers just as you'll always live in my heart. I know they'll love you too.

For my daughter, Stephanie, thank you for allowing me to include you as a character in my story. Your bravery and love keep me going even on the darkest days.

Finally, for Joyce Maynard and all of the amazing women writers who sat with me in the 2014 writers' circle under the volcanoes by Lake Atitlan in Guatemala, you gave me my voice back after grief had rendered me speechless.

ABOUT THE AUTHOR

 **Mary Jane Black** studied English and journalism as an undergrad, and went on to pursue a master's in English with a concentration in creative writing. She left her writing degree program to accept a job teaching high school English when she became a solo mom with a teenage daughter. She taught writing and literature in high schools for fourteen years, and is currently a literary specialist for the State of Texas. Excerpts from her memoir appeared in the July 2016 issue of *Shark Reef Journal* and in the August 2016 issue of *American Oxford* magazine. *She Rode a Harley* is Black's first book.

SELECTED TITLES
FROM SHE WRITES PRESS

She Writes Press is an independent publishing company
founded to serve women writers everywhere.
Visit us at www.shewritespress.com.

Letting Go into Perfect Love: Discovering the Extraordinary After Abuse by Gwendolyn M. Plano. $16.95, 978-1-938314-74-2. After staying in an abusive marriage for twenty-five years, Gwen Plano finally broke free—and started down the long road toward healing.

Lost in the Reflecting Pool: A Memoir by Diane Pomerantz. $16.95, 978-1-63152-268-0. A psychological story about Diane, a highly trained child psychologist, who falls in love with Charles, a brilliant and charming psychiatrist—ignoring all the red flags that will later come back to haunt her.

Loveyoubye: Holding Fast, Letting Go, And Then There's The Dog by Rossandra White. $16.95, 978-1-938314-50-6. A soul-searching memoir detailing the painful, but ultimately liberating, disintegration of a twenty-five-year marriage.

Miracle at Midlife: A Transatlantic Romance by Roni Beth Tower. $16.95, 978-1-63152-123-2. An inspiring memoir chronicling the sudden, unexpected, and life-changing two-year courtship between a divorced American lawyer living on a houseboat in the center of Paris and an empty-nested clinical psychologist living in Connecticut.

Naked Mountain: A Memoir by Marcia Mabee. $16.95, 978-1-63152-097-6. A compelling memoir of one woman's journey of natural world discovery, tragedy, and the enduring bonds of marriage, set against the backdrop of a stunning mountaintop in rural Virginia.

Gap Year Girl by Marianne Bohr. $16.95, 978-1-63152-820-0. Thirty-plus years after first backpacking through Europe, Marianne Bohr and her husband leave their lives behind and take off on a yearlong quest for adventure.

SHE RODE
A HARLEY